# John Gurda's
# MILWAUKEE

*A Self-Guided Historical Tour*

# Introduction

**M**ilwaukee is a city that rewards exploration. Its street system is a straightforward Midwestern grid, its traffic is famously manageable, and its downtown is built at the human scale. But it's not just logistical ease that makes touring the city a pleasure. Milwaukee's personality is an intriguing blend of large and small. It combines big-league attractions with the ease and approachability of a much smaller community, and you'll find remarkable diversity, both cultural and architectural, in an invitingly compact landscape. That hybrid character enables visitors to develop a fuller understanding of Milwaukee in a half-day than they could learn about many cities in a week.

*John Gurda's Milwaukee* is a grassroots introduction to the riches of this hometown metropolis. Although the route includes plenty of well-known attractions—the Art Museum, the Summerfest grounds, grand churches and, yes, historic breweries—the emphasis is on the human side of the city rather than its institutional expressions. You'll see where Milwaukeeans live, work, and re-create —a grittier but ultimately more authentic view than the approved scenes on the postcards in the airport gift shop.

Studying Milwaukee has been my full-time job since 1972, a largely unplanned but thoroughly gratifying career. Most of what I've learned has found its way into books, articles, and documentaries, but tours emerged early on as another way to tell Milwaukee's story, and the city itself has been an incomparable visual aid. I began to lead bus tours in the mid-1970s, and I've shared my hometown with thousands of people since then—Junior Leaguers, business leaders, neighborhood residents, foreign visitors, public officials, conventioneers, journalists, young lawyers, schoolkids, family groups, and a host of others. I developed, over the years, a route that reveals Milwaukee, not necessarily at its best, but at its most characteristic. Here you'll find Polish flats and German duplexes, reclaimed mansions and public housing projects, all set in neighborhoods that range from challenged to charmed.

A word about navigation. The route is necessarily linear, but it divides neatly into roughly fifteen distinct neighborhood segments, each with its major points of interest highlighted by number both in the text and on an accompanying map. The entire tour covers about twenty-five miles and takes a leisurely morning or afternoon to complete by car. Purposely low-tech, it's guaranteed to refresh the map-reading skills of a generation raised on GPS. Although most users will probably drive, the route is eminently bikeable, and navigation is much easier on two wheels than four. If you do drive, don't try it alone. The only safe way to enjoy this tour by car is to have one person at the wheel and another navigating and narrating.

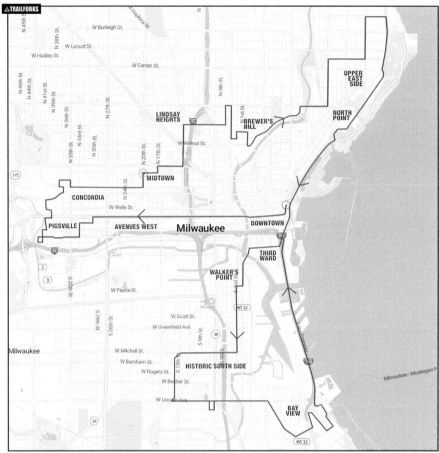

*The tour route inscribes a contorted figure-eight on the heart of the city, running clockwise through neighborhoods north of the Menomonee Valley and counterclockwise to the south.*

*John Gurda's Milwaukee* is the vehicle I've chosen to transfer a good deal of hard-won knowledge from the recesses of my aging brain to a permanent place in the public domain. It's also a snapshot of Milwaukee in the 2020s. Someone who discovers this tour on a dusty shelf decades from now will likely find it curiously antique, a yellowing testament to a city lost to memory. I welcome that fate as confirmation that cities, like the people they serve, are constantly in motion, forever evolving in directions that defy easy understanding. As you explore Milwaukee in the here and now, I hope the experience heightens your appreciation of a city undersung but utterly distinctive, and one that's moving, always moving, from a fixed past to an indeterminate future at the constant speed of life.

*John Gurda*

# Downtown

*The tour starts at The Cudahy, a 1909 condo tower at 777 N. Prospect Ave. Park or pull over on Prospect anywhere between Wells and Mason Streets.*

A ny self-respecting tour of Milwaukee has to start within sight of Lake Michigan. The city is perched on one of the largest bodies of freshwater on earth, part of a system that holds twenty percent of the planet's fresh surface water. The five Great Lakes are a globally important resource, but Lake Michigan has played an especially important role in Milwaukee's development. It is the source of our drinking water, a major influence on our weather, a magnet for recreation and, in the longest view, the reason for the city's existence. In the early years of urban settlement, anyone who got here, got here by boat. The typical traveler made it first to Albany, New York, took the Erie Canal across the state to Buffalo, and then boarded a schooner (later a steamship) all the way to the south end of Lake Michigan.

With its broad bay and deep river, Milwaukee had the best natural harbor on the western shore of the lake. That made the little fur trading post a premier urban opportunity and a formidable competitor with Chicago, which was handicapped by its inferior harbor and its position at the dead end of the lake. The two settlements were neck and neck in population for more than fifteen years—from 1835, the date of Milwaukee's first land sale, until 1852, when the first railroad entered Chicago from the east. Lake Michigan forced rail traffic to its southern end, changing the regional balance of power forever. Chicago quickly became the "Freight Handler to the Nation" and the second-largest city in America. Milwaukee was the runner-up in the region, but it became a metropolis in its own right, earning its first prosperity as the largest shipper of wheat on earth. The harbor is *why* Milwaukee is, and why Milwaukee is *where* it is.

*Pull out onto Prospect Ave. As you head west through downtown, stay in the right lane and slow down enough to catch multiple red lights.*

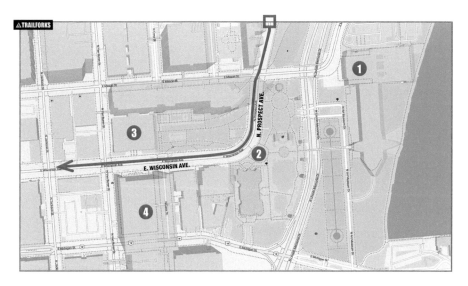

*The lakefront has been Milwaukee's showplace since the first bluffside park welcomed visitors in the 1880s.*

The **Milwaukee County War Memorial Center**, ❶ the landmark at the foot of Mason Street, is one of the city's most significant mid-century modern buildings. Dedicated in 1957, it's the work of Eero Saarinen, the celebrated Finnish-American architect. The colorful mosaic on its facade incorporates the beginning and ending dates of World War II and the Korean Conflict, whose veterans the center was built to honor. Today it houses a number of veterans service groups and, on the lower levels, a major portion of the Milwaukee Art Museum's collection.

The orange sunburst at the bend in the road is Mark di Suvero's ***The Calling***,❷ probably the best-known and certainly the most controversial public sculpture in Milwaukee. I like to think of it as an asterisk on Milwaukee's lakefront, punctuating the spectacular view. As you turn onto Wisconsin Avenue, the city's main drag, you'll see on the right the biggest financial institution in Wisconsin and the largest individual life insurer in America: **Northwestern Mutual Life**.❸ The company was founded in Janesville in 1857 and moved to Milwaukee just two years later. In 1914, after outgrowing a number of smaller buildings on or near E. Wisconsin Avenue, Northwestern built an updated version of a Greek temple at the corner of Van Buren Street as its home office. The campus has been expanding ever since. The biggest addition by far is Northwestern Mutual Tower and Commons, which opened in 2017 as a $450 million investment in the future of the company and its adopted hometown. It's now the second-tallest building on our skyline. One perk NM has offered since 1914 is an excellent free lunch for all employees. It's a great amenity, but free food also keeps NM's workers on campus, interacting, and engaged—an important factor in the post-pandemic workplace.

Directly across from Northwestern Mutual, and literally overshadowing it, is the **US Bank building**,❹ which opened in 1973 as the headquarters of First Wisconsin Bank. Although it would get lost in Chicago's Loop, US Bank is, at 601 feet and 42 stories, the tallest building in Wisconsin. The skyscraper rose during the administration of CEO George Kasten, who made it his main pre-retirement project. As his career neared its sunset, Kasten spent more and more time working on the building. Some of his less-reverent friends took to calling it "George's last erection."

### Proceed from Van Buren to Water St.

The procession of landmarks on E. Wisconsin Avenue continues west of Van Buren. On the right is the **Wisconsin Gas** building,❺ a 1930 creation that is among Milwaukee's finest examples of the Art Deco style. Its crowning glory is an illuminated flame that tells the weather, although the color code is less than intuitive. Gold represents cold, red predicts "warm weather ahead," and blue signifies "no change in view," while a blinking light indicates precipitation.

On the left at Jackson Street is the old **Federal Building**,❻ which was built in stages during the 1890s. It was Milwaukee's main post office for many years but now houses only courtrooms and administrative offices. The interior of this graceful Richardsonian Romanesque landmark has been thoroughly restored, and it's well worth putting up with the metal detectors to pay a visit.

Directly across from the Federal Building, adorned with one of Milwaukee's few remaining street clocks, stands the original home of **Northwestern National Insurance,** a property and casualty firm founded by Alexander Mitchell, whom you'll meet again soon. It's now a branch of the Northern Trust Company.

Just past Jefferson Street on the right is the **Pfister Hotel,** which opened in 1893. Virtually every American president since William McKinley has stayed in what is generally considered the grande dame of Milwaukee's hotels. The Pfister is also a great example of historic preservation at work, one of many in downtown Milwaukee. If you glance down some of the side streets, especially to the south down **Broadway,** you'll see streetscapes that have changed relatively little in the last century.

*East Wisconsin Avenue was a sea of humanity at the turn of the twentieth century.*

## Try to catch a red light at Water St.

On the left at Water Street, you'll see a one-of-a-kind commercial building: the **Iron Block**, which is faced with cast-iron sections shipped from New York and bolted together on the site, a little like Legos. Completed in 1861, it's one of Milwaukee's relatively few pre-Civil War buildings. A much newer landmark is the green-glass Chase Tower on the left, which was built in 1962 as the **Marine Bank**. Founded in 1839, the Marine was Wisconsin's first bank, and its guiding light was Alexander Mitchell, our pioneer tycoon.

On the north side of the Water Street intersection is the site of Solomon Juneau's **fur trading post**. He and his wife, Josette, moved here in 1825 because this location offered the first dependably dry ground above the mouth of the Milwaukee River; everything downstream was a swamp. To this day, the corner of Water and Wisconsin is downtown Milwaukee's commercial crossroads, a role it has been playing ever since Solomon Juneau's time.

## Start crossing the Wisconsin Ave. bridge

*Angled bridges have been a fixture of downtown Milwaukee since the city's infancy. This humble span dates from 1870.*

MILWAUKEE JOURNAL SENTINEL

Much of what you'll be seeing on this tour is neighborhoods, and their history in Milwaukee begins early. The pioneer settlement east of the river was called Juneautown, honoring, of course, the community's last fur trader and first mayor. The district west of the river was named Kilbourntown, after Byron Kilbourn, a Connecticut-born Yankee who settled there in 1834. The two sides didn't get along, a fact immortalized in our **downtown bridges**. Kilbourn laid out his street system completely independent of Juneau's. When bridges were finally built, they crossed the river at an angle, a civic antique that's still with us.

The two sides actually came to blows over the issue of bridges. In 1840, despite Byron Kilbourn's spirited objections, Juneautown had a bridge built several blocks north of here at Chestnut Street (now Juneau Avenue, ironically). The west siders suffered in silence for a time, but one warm night in May of 1845, they used axes and saws to liberate their end of the bridge, which collapsed into the river and blocked all northbound boat traffic. Juneautown partisans reacted by cutting off Kilbourntown's bridges to the south, and soon a small-scale war was under way. There were no fatalities, but blood was spilled in this comic-opera conflict; the *Milwaukee Sentinel* reported that a few combatants were "considerably injured, though not dangerously." Both sides finally realized that a civil war was poor advertising for a frontier town trying to attract settlers. On January 31, 1846, the two sides came together as the City of Milwaukee, taking in Walker's Point on the south side as well. The Great Bridge War ended with the incorporation of the first city in Wisconsin.

## Cross Plankinton Ave.

The block-long building on the left is the elegant **Plankinton Arcade,** 🔞 which was built in 1916 as a shopping center on the European model. In 1982 the Arcade became a central link in the Grand Avenue Mall, a "festival marketplace" that stretched from Gimbels on the Milwaukee River all the way to Boston Store on Fourth Street. The Grand Avenue was the busiest retail complex in the state for several years, until it was overtaken by suburban malls and big boxes. Most of the former mall's buildings have been converted to housing and offices, but a food court is still one of its major features.

The oversized "WARNER" sign at 212 W. Wisconsin identifies a landmark that has had two incarnations in two centuries. The Warner Theater was Milwaukee's most lavish movie palace from the night it opened in 1931 until it went dark in 1995. After a top-to-bottom restoration, the 2500-seat theater reopened in 2021 as the **Bradley Symphony Center,** 🔞 the new (and acoustically superb) home of the Milwaukee Symphony Orchestra, completing a transition from Bogart to Beethoven.

Directly across Martin Luther King Drive (N. Third Street) is the **310W Building,** 🔞 an office structure that opened in 1983 as the Reuss Federal Plaza, providing space for several federal agencies. The cobalt blue glass exterior has suggested an alternate name: the Milk of Magnesia Building.

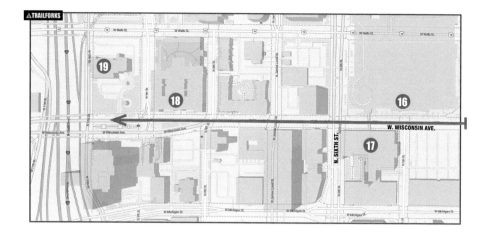

The massive structure in the next block is the **Baird Center** 🔟 (formerly the Wisconsin Center), Milwaukee's major convention facility. It's part of a historic complex of gathering places that extends three blocks north to Fiserv Forum. On the left at Fifth Street is the **Hilton Milwaukee City Center,** 🔟 which was built in 1927 as the Schroeder Hotel. It's the largest hostelry in Milwaukee and the city's largest Art Deco structure as well.

## *Cross Sixth St.*

The skyline drops off precipitously west of Sixth Street, the start of a low-rise zone that extends for miles. For a metro area of 1.6 million people, Milwaukee doesn't have an especially imposing downtown. One explanation is that there were multiple "downtowns" in the residential neighborhoods, robust commercial corridors that served their respective regions of the city. To illustrate the point, Schuster's was the largest department store chain in the state, and it had no downtown location. All of its business was done in stores on N. Third, Mitchell, and Vliet Streets.

What they lack in stature, several of the buildings west of Sixth make up for in grandeur. One of my favorites is the **Central Library,** 🔟 which opened in 1898 as a combination library and museum. The two institutions were like twins developing in the same womb, jostling for space as they grew. The crowding continued until the museum moved to the north side of Wells Street in the mid-1960s, allowing the library to take over the entire building.

## *Pull over in front of the Wisconsin Club.*

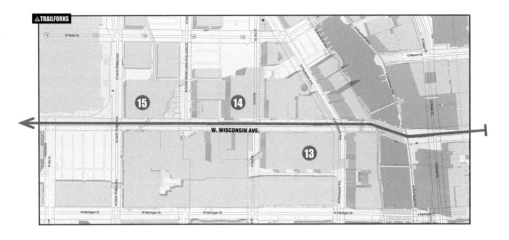

This palatial structure was once a single-family home, and the lord of the manor was **Alexander Mitchell.⑲** You've already seen two of his businesses—Northwestern National Insurance and the Marine Bank—and a third was even larger: the Milwaukee Road, Wisconsin's major rail line. Mitchell was a canny Scotsman who came to Milwaukee in 1839 and proceeded to make himself the richest man in the state. Early in his career, the immigrant bought an unpretentious brick home on this site. As his fortune grew, he enlarged its dimensions and created a Victorian showplace, with hand-tooled wall coverings, parquet floors, lots of stained glass, and a front-yard conservatory in which he grew everything from orchids to pineapples.

Following the tycoon's death in 1887, his home was first rented and then purchased by a group of affluent Germans who had banded together as the Deutscher Club. It is difficult to overstate the impact of Milwaukee's German settlers. They were a majority of the population as early as 1860, and the group played a formative role in the city's economic, political, and cultural life. This is where the city's Teutonic elite raised their steins, bowled their tenpins in a new alley, and married off their sons and daughters. The mansion remained a center of *Gemütlichkeit*—relaxed fellowship—until the United States entered World War I in 1917, which made it instantly impolitic to be waving the German flag. The Deutscher Club became the Wisconsin Club, and so it has been ever since.

In Alexander Mitchell's day, W. Wisconsin Avenue was called Spring Street, a reference to the springs that flowed from the bluff to the east. The street was renamed Grand Avenue in 1876 because it was fast becoming a district of grand homes like Mitchell's. His mansion set the tone for a residential gold coast that extended all the way to the Menomonee Valley at Thirty-ninth Street.

# *Avenues West*

Crossing Interstate 43, you move from downtown to the Near West Side, specifically the Avenues West neighborhood. The district's largest institution is Marquette University, whose campus begins literally at the freeway. Marquette was founded by the Jesuits, a prominent Catholic teaching order, in 1881, but not in this location. Its first home was on the State Street hill near Tenth Street, which is why the school's early athletic teams were known as the Hilltoppers. MU moved to Grand Avenue in 1907, building **Johnston Hall ❶** at what is now 1131 W. Wisconsin. Johnston was the entire campus, the first structure in a complex that now covers well over 100 acres.

Immediately west of Johnston Hall is Marquette's most conspicuous landmark: **Gesu Church.❷** Most Milwaukeeans think of it as a campus institution today, but Gesu was actually dedicated in 1894 as the parish church for a heavily Irish neighborhood called Tory Hill, which sprawled across the hillside south of Grand Avenue. I've described the Marquette Interchange as Milwaukee's largest tombstone, because it rests directly atop the buried remains of Tory Hill.

Marquette University now serves a student body of more than 11,000 with degree programs in engineering, nursing, dentistry, law, and the liberal arts—and its basketball team isn't bad either. MU is a major Milwaukee cultural institution, but it's also a great example of the "brain gain" often associated with large universities. A significant number of graduates come to Milwaukee for college and stay to become productive and often prominent citizens.

Not that Marquette has always escaped controversy. The **Alumni Memorial Union ❸** (1442 W. Wisconsin) stands on the site of an opulent mansion built in about 1890 for Elizabeth Plankinton, the heiress of an affluent meat-packing family. On a fall weekend in 1980, when news coverage was at its lightest, Marquette demolished the mansion to make way for its student union. Enraged preservationists mounted a successful campaign for stricter safeguards for the city's most historic buildings.

## *Cross 17th St.*

The theme just west of Seventeenth Street is health care, both past and present. The major institutions are **Versiti Blood Center ❹** and **Humphrey Residence Hall ❺** at Seventeenth and the **MU Dental School ❻** at Eighteenth. Humphrey Hall was once Children's Hospital, and the Dental School rests on the site of Deaconess Hospital (my birthplace). They were just two of eight hospitals on the Near West Side that provided abundant and easily accessible learning opportunities for students at Marquette's medical school, which continues an independent existence as the Medical College of Wisconsin in suburban Wauwatosa.

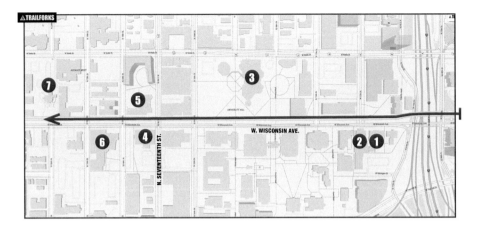

*Johnston Hall was Marquette University's entire campus in 1907. Gesu Church is visible on the right.*

*Both inside and out, the home of meatpacker John Plankinton was a Grand Avenue showplace. Parasol in hand, Anna Plankinton was queen of the seven-acre kingdom.*

## Pull over in front of Pabst Mansion, 2000 W. Wisconsin

West Wisconsin Avenue's days as a gold coast are obviously over, but the **Pabst Mansion ❼** is a vivid reminder of the street's affluent heyday. This Victorian standout was built for Capt. Frederick Pabst and his family in 1892, when Pabst's brewery was the largest in America. Their home is the only Grand Avenue mansion that's not only still standing but also open to the public. If you want to see how beer barons lived in the days before the income tax, here's a great place to vicariously experience spectacular wealth. Christmas is an especially festive time, but the Pabst Mansion can also be rented for weddings, corporate events, and other gatherings.

The Pabst is a distinguished survivor. The only reason the building is still here is that it was the official residence of Milwaukee's Catholic archbishops for decades, from Sebastian Messmer in 1908 to William Cousins in 1975. When Cousins departed for the suburbs, a developer purchased the home and announced plans to replace it with a parking lot. By that time, fortunately, the preservation movement was gaining traction—a development that dates to roughly 1970, both nationally and locally. A nonprofit group was formed to acquire the mansion, and year by year, room by room, detail by detail, the organization has restored the Pabst to its original elegance, making it without question Milwaukee's favorite house museum.

## Continue west on Wisconsin Ave.

Why did so few Grand Avenue mansions survive? It was a matter of supply and demand. As Milwaukee's population soared after 1900, so did the demand for housing near the heart of town. People wanted a foothold close to the center of things, and the Near West Side filled the bill. Wealthy families felt the pressure and left. One by one, their mansions were cut up into small apartments or replaced by large apartment buildings, particularly in the Teens and Twenties.

And where did the rich folks go? They headed west, many to the Concordia neighborhood you'll see shortly, and their descendants kept moving west to Washington Heights, Washington Highlands, Wauwatosa, Elm Grove, and Brookfield. I often describe history as why things are the way they are, and you see that pattern clearly in the landscape west of downtown. A corridor of affluent settlement spanning more than a century extends in one unbroken line from the Mitchell mansion on Ninth and Wisconsin to brand-new "McMansions" in the Town of Brookfield.

The former church at 2133 W. Wisconsin is a survivor with a story. Grand Avenue Congregational Church was built in 1888 to serve affluent Yankee families on the Near West Side. The congregation's ranks thinned as the neighborhood changed, but it remained viable until the end of the twentieth century. In 1996 title finally passed to a coalition of Irish groups who repurposed the building as the **Irish Cultural and Heritage Center, ❽** a leading venue for Irish music and Irish organizational life.

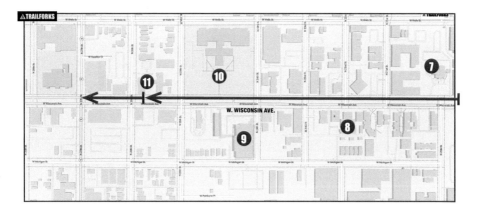

There was a powerful but little-noticed symbolism in the change of ownership. Milwaukee's Irish population had long been confined to the working-class neighborhoods south of Grand Avenue. Taking over a Romanesque landmark built by well-heeled Yankees on the Avenue itself was equivalent to moving uptown. After generations in the socio-economic shadows, Irish Milwaukeeans had gained a symbolic foothold on the city's old gold coast, and the ICHC remains an anchor of Celtic pride today.

A variety of other organizations found homes on the Avenue. A menagerie of fraternal groups came to life in America at the turn of the twentieth century, among them the Elks, the Moose, the Lions, the Owls, and the Eagles. In 1926 Milwaukee's **Eagles** ❾ built the lavish clubhouse at 2401 W. Wisconsin. Its major attraction was George Devine's Million Dollar Ballroom, the state's largest dance floor and a popular stop for the era's big bands. Recent years have threatened every species of fraternal group with extinction. The Eagles have flown, and their classic clubhouse is now the home of the Rave, a venue for music far removed from Tommy Dorsey and Benny Goodman. The building across the street opened in 1930 as Milwaukee County's **Downtown Emergency Hospital.** ❿ It now houses the Academy of Chinese Language, one of several Milwaukee public schools with a language specialty.

### Pull over east of 2532 W. Wisconsin

The **oddly hybrid structure** ⓫ at 2532 W. Wisconsin illustrates in one location the rise and fall of Grand Avenue as a gold coast. It was built in 1897 as a mansion for Gerhard Winner, a German immigrant who made his fortune as a liquor distiller and wholesaler. After Winner's death in 1906, his home was stripped of its oak paneling and marble bathrooms and cut up into eighteen "furnished rooms." Worse yet, an auto dealer tacked a two-story addition onto the front of the home in 1952 and used it to showcase his used cars. A fry shop and a check-cashing business occupy the addition today, like barnacles of modern commerce encrusting a worn reminder of Grand Avenue in its heyday.

# Merrill Park

Crossing Twenty-seventh Street, you enter the first exclusively residential neighborhood west of downtown: Merrill Park. It's also one of the most crisply defined neighborhoods in the city, a rectangle bordered by Wisconsin Avenue and Interstate 94 between Twenty-seventh and Thirty-fifth Streets. There was a Merrill—Sherburn S. —and he worked for Alexander Mitchell as general manager of the Milwaukee Road. It was apparently Merrill's decision to move the railroad's main shops to the Menomonee Valley west of Thirty-fifth Street in 1880. Those shops became an employment magnet that pulled hundreds of Irish families, in particular, to the western city limits. Merrill owned a gentleman's farm, complete with a mansion on Grand Avenue, that covered most of the future neighborhood. He employed a majority of the newcomers and sold them lots as well, ending his days with an estate valued at just under $1 million.

## Turn left on 30th St.

As you start to turn left on Thirtieth, you can hardly miss the colorful building on the right. It's the **Tripoli Shrine,** ❶ Milwaukee's own Taj Mahal, sort of. It was built in 1926 as the clubhouse for a Masonic fraternal group known as the Shriners, the fez-wearing, fun-loving guys you see piloting synchronized go-karts in civic parades and putting on the Shrine Circus. Their one-of-a-kind landmark is now available for rentals.

## Turn right on Michigan St. and pull over.

There were German and Yankee families in Merrill Park, but the largest single group traced its origins to Ireland, and their most important institution was **St. Rose of Lima Church,** ❷ which was dedicated in 1888. The roster of charter members read like the Dublin phone book, filled with names like Kelly, Murphy, O'Toole, and O'Brien. St. Rose was such a prominent landmark and such a beehive of activity that Merrill Park was widely identified as Milwaukee's premier Irish neighborhood.

The St. Rose campus covers nearly a square block, and its size is due in part to a quirk of geography. The parish boundaries extended north to include the Concordia neighborhood, which, as you'll soon see, was a center of affluence. There were, by one count, nineteen millionaires on the rolls in the 1920s, none of them living below Grand Avenue. Staunch Catholics like the Millers of brewing fame may not have attended the school plays or the Holy Name Society smokers, but they gave generously at fundraising time, enabling an Irish working-class parish to build a school with a double gym and a double auditorium.

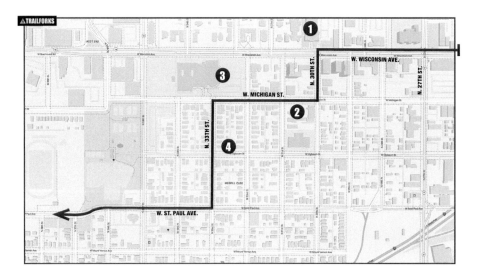

*As general manager of the state's largest railroad, Sherburn S. Merrill could afford a lavish home on Grand Avenue in the neighborhood that still bears his name.*

### Continue west on Michigan St.

Most of the houses in Merrill Park date from the turn of the twentieth century, particularly between 1890 and 1910. The neighborhood's largest institution put down roots in 1925: **Marquette University High School,** ❸ a Catholic boys' school run by the Jesuit teaching order. Not surprisingly, a sizable proportion of its graduates move down the avenue to Marquette University after graduation. This was once Sherburn S. Merrill's land, and his Grand Avenue mansion rested on the present site of Marquette High's cafeteria.

*Completed in 1888, St. Rose Church was the social and spiritual hub of Merrill Park's Irish community.*

*The Irish Village was another community anchor and the neighborhood's only tavern, located just outside S.S. Merrill's alcohol-free zone. (right) Mayor Frank Zeidler, who led the city from 1948 to 1960, was a proud son of Merrill Park.*

## Turn left on 33rd St.

In the 1970s, Marquette bought most of the homes in this block and made plans to replace them with an athletic field. The preservation movement was under way by then, and the school decided to help the cause rather than fight it. The homes were sold to the Westside Conservation Corporation of blessed memory, who rehabbed them inside and out and sold them to owner-occupants.

The house at 504, at the end of the block, was the boyhood home of two Milwaukee mayors: the **Zeidler brothers.** ❹ The first was Carl, a charismatic city attorney who won the mayor's office in 1940 and was lost at sea during World War II. His younger brother, Frank, served three terms, from 1948 to 1960, as the last Socialist to govern a major American city—or, as he might have preferred to say, the most recent. Their father, Mike, was a barber who cut hair near the Marquette University campus well into his eighties. The Zeidlers were one of the relatively few German families in a heavily Irish neighborhood.

## Cross Clybourn St.

There's notable variety in the housing stock as you head south, including a large number of duplexes. There's also ample evidence of rehabilitation, and obvious potential for a lot more. One thing you will not see in Merrill Park today is taverns. Sherburn Merrill was a teetotaling Yankee who put a deed restriction into every property he sold that prohibited the sale or manufacture of alcoholic beverages. A smart lawyer could probably break that provision today but, on land originally owned by Merrill, east of Thirty-fifth Street and west of Thirtieth, there is not, and never has been, a single saloon. The result is an Irish neighborhood without taverns—a living oxymoron.

## Turn right on St. Paul Ave.

One of Merrill Park's hallmarks in the twenty-first century is its ethnic diversity; the neighborhood's residents include Blacks, Latinos, Asians, Native Americans, and even a few holdover Irish families. No single group predominates, and the result is that Merrill Park is one of the most successfully integrated neighborhoods in Milwaukee.

# Pigsville

Crossing Thirty-fifth Street, you leave Merrill Park behind and approach the smallest neighborhood in Milwaukee: Pigsville. Notice what happens as you travel west. First you pass the green space of the **Merrill Park playfield ❶** and then, at the bottom of the hill, you see **Quad Park,❷** Marquette High's track and soccer facility and the former site of Marquette University's football stadium. Until it was discontinued in 1960, MU's marquee sport was not basketball but football; the school played in the 1937 Cotton Bowl, losing to Texas Christian University. The continuous green space west of Thirty-fifth creates a buffer zone between Merrill Park, up on the hill, and Pigsville, down here in the valley, creating a strong sense of separation between the communities.

### Cross 39th St.

Pigsville is not only the smallest neighborhood in Milwaukee, but it's also the most isolated and without doubt the most unusually named. There are fewer than 300 households here and only eleven streets, seven of which end in dead ends. Very few people come to Pigsville unless they live here or they're lost.

As you can see, the houses are more modest than those in Merrill Park, but they tend to be somewhat better maintained. Most were built at about the same time as Merrill Park's, and by the same class of industrial workers who were moving west to jobs in the Menomonee Valley or Miller Valley. But there were practically no Irish families here. Germans were among the first to arrive, but they were eventually outnumbered by eastern Europeans, including Poles, Russians, Serbs, and especially Slovaks. This was one of the major Slovak neighborhoods in Milwaukee, and a few families have been in the valley for generations.

### Turn left at 42nd St. and pull over.

It seems appropriate that Milwaukee's smallest neighborhood has one of its smallest parks. **Valley Park ❸** is just as public a green space as Lake or Grant or Whitnall, but it exists largely for the enjoyment of people from this neighborhood. Milwaukee County does have an extraordinary park system: 15,000 acres of green space, about five times per capita more than the city of Chicago. Park development in the county was led by a Socialist named Charles Whitnall, who believed that everyone should live within walking distance of a park to feel the uplifting influence of nature. Valley Park is a great example of that policy's success.

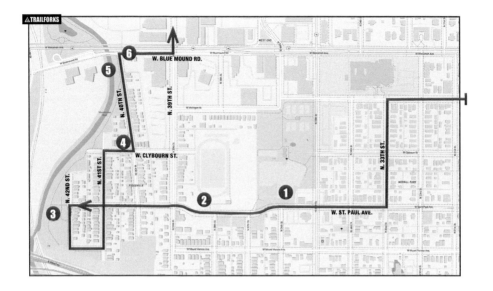

Many of Pigsville's homes are a type called the Polish flat, which you'll see in greater abundance on the South Side. They represent entry-level worker housing, paid for with wages from nearby industrial employers, including the Milwaukee Road.

### Turn left on Mt. Vernon Ave. and left again on 41st.

And the name? There are multiple theories about the origin of "Pigsville." One is that a man named George Pigg—two "g"s—had a popular inn on Blue Mound Road during the stagecoach era. Another, more creative explanation is that trains bringing pork to market from Wisconsin farms sometimes derailed as they made the sharp turn at the entrance to the valley, allowing the pigs to wander up into the surrounding neighborhood. A related story is that high water occasionally washed pigs off their farms in Wauwatosa when the Menomonee River flooded. When the current slowed at the river's bend, they would clamber up onto the banks. Yet another theory is that local residents roasted pigs in their backyards, but that was true in any number of immigrant neighborhoods.

In 1980 I wrote a book called *The West End* about three West Side neighborhoods—Merrill Park, Pigsville, and Concordia—and I was determined to track down the origin of the name. I finally met a woman named Mary Lemanski, whose family had been among the first to settle here. As the Lemanskis and others were putting down roots on the east side of the river, the west bank was occupied by the farm of a family named Freis, whose specialty was pigs. Not surprisingly, the developing neighborhood was soon associated with the animals. The name "Pigstown" appeared in print for the first time in 1894 and eventually morphed to "Pigsville."

*A major highway today, Blue Mound Road was a rutted country lane when it passed through Pigsville in the 1800s.*

It's likely that residents heard enough snickering over the years that some loyalist invented a George Pigg—two "g"s—to give the neighbor just a little more prestige, or at least a less firm association with pork on the hoof. You'll still encounter both spellings, but P-I-G is the historically correct alternative.

### *Turn right on Clybourn St. and left on 40th St.*

The tavern on the corner of Fortieth Street is the **Valley Inn,** ❹ which has been in the same family since 1955. For most of the twentieth century, Pigsville was practically a self-contained community, with its own grocery stores, bakeries, butcher shops, and saloons. This is the last business remaining, and it's about as neighborhood a bar as you'll find in Milwaukee. It's also a great place for lunch or dinner if you're seeking a uniquely down-home place to enjoy a meal.

### *Pull over on 40th St. just south of Blue Mound Rd.*

And that's Pigsville. You've seen virtually the entire neighborhood, but there's a final grace note in the landscape. If you look to the left, the **Menomonee River** ❺ is just below you, winding its way into the city from Menomonee Falls and points beyond. The river has been an unpredictable neighbor from the very beginning.

Periodic floods would fill basements and carry away garages, which led to various water control projects, two of them visible between you and American Family Field. The weathered walls closest to the river level were built by federal work relief crews during the Depression. The Menomonee still flooded, and a much higher levee was completed in 2001 by the Milwaukee Metropolitan Sewerage District. So far, so good. The flooding has been contained, at least to date, even in these times of climate change.

## Turn right on Blue Mound Rd. and left on 39th St.

Blue Mound Road ❻ in Pigsville is the same Blue Mound Road that many Milwaukeeans probably associate with the eight-lane corridor of commerce in suburban Brookfield. In the mid-1800s, this was the main-traveled road from Milwaukee to all points due west, and it remained so until an earlier version of this bridge was built across the Menomonee Valley in 1911. The Grand Avenue viaduct put a roof over the neighborhood and allowed it to develop in peace and quiet, and that's the way it's been ever since. Pigsville is probably the closest thing Milwaukee has to an urban village. It's hardly a Brigadoon that time forgot, and the neighborhood is much more diverse, racially and economically, than it ever has been, but Pigsville remains a community with an extraordinarily strong sense of place—and a most unusual name.

In 1911 all through traffic shifted from the valley floor to the new Grand Avenue viaduct.

# Miller Valley

Passing beneath the new (1993) Wisconsin Avenue viaduct, you move from Milwaukee's smallest neighborhood to one of America's largest breweries. This is the birthplace of **Miller Brewing,❶** now part of Molson Coors. As visitors learn on the official tour, it was founded in 1849 as the Plank Road Brewery by two Best brothers, Charles and Lorenz, whose family also launched what is now Pabst Brewing. The Bests failed to prosper here, and in 1855 their bankrupt brewery was purchased by Frederick Miller, a German immigrant who had crossed the ocean with $9000 in gold on his person. That was enough to parlay his successful European brewery career into an even more successful one here. Miller quickly reopened and expanded the business, and his creation is still going strong as part of a national conglomerate.

## Pause just south of State St.

As you near the heart of the brewing complex, there is literally beer flowing across the street high above you. The **pipes overhead ❷** run from I House on the right to Miller's packaging center on the left in two primary streams: Miller High Life, which can also become Miller Genuine Draft (it's the same beer but filtered differently), and Miller Lite. Oceans of suds cross this street every year, including beers brewed under contract for old rivals Pabst and Schlitz.

## Turn right on State St.

State Street opened in 1848 as the Watertown Plank Road, providing the brewery with its original name. Even though he was well beyond the city limits at first, Fred Miller earned a reputation for quality that made his company a Milwaukee powerhouse. It was not, however, until a century later, in the 1950s, that Miller became a national brewer, a shift that occurred under the founder's charismatic grandson, Frederick C. Miller.

Company landmarks pass in quick succession as you head east. The **Miller Inn ❸** (3931 State) is the brewery's hospitality center and a popular event venue. It adjoins the entrance to the **caves ❹** that were created to cool Miller's finest in the years before mechanical refrigeration. Directly across the street is the Brooks Stevens-designed **corporate headquarters ❺** that opened in 1951. The **frame building ❻** perched on the hillside above the caves entrance is actually part of a movie set built to celebrate the company's centennial in 1955. It marks the eastern entrance to Miller Valley.

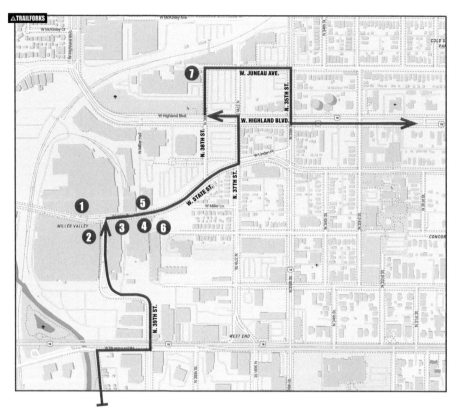

*Miller Brewing was a major Milwaukee producer by the date of this 1892 lithograph.*

*Turn left on 37th St. and left again on Highland Blvd. Pull over just before 38th St.*

As you climb the hill to Highland Boulevard, you're entering the newer section of Miller's campus. For generations the company was content to stay in the valley, but a fateful merger led to explosive growth. In 1969, after a period of general drift and uncertainty, Miller was sold to Philip Morris. The tobacco giant had seen the handwriting on the wall. Public scrutiny of its addictive, carcinogenic main product was growing, and the company was diversifying its holdings in response. Philip Morris had already earned a reputation for masterful marketing. Marlboro, for instance, was initially sold as a ladies' cigarette, but Philip Morris tied its fortunes to the rugged, free-range Marlboro Man and made the brand the best-selling in America.

The new parent was determined to work the same magic in the brewing industry. In 1972 Miller bought three brands from a struggling Chicago brewery named Meister Brau. One of them was Lite, which had been marketed as a diet beer for women. Just as they had with Marlboro, Philip Morris's marketers masculinized the product. They hired what seemed to be every retired sports star in America and featured them in an endless series of ads pitting "Tastes Great" against "Less Filling." Saturation advertising made Miller Lite the company's best-selling beer by a wide margin, and it dominated an entirely new category. Between 1969 and 1977, largely on the strength of Lite, Miller's sales volume surged from seventh place in America's brewing industry to second, trailing only Anheuser-Busch. Miller was growing so fast in the 1970s that the company built a new headquarters building here on Highland—the one at the end of the block—and had to put up another before the first was even fully occupied.

The theme in more recent years has been global consolidation. In 2002 Philip Morris sold its Miller subsidiary to South African Breweries, creating an international conglomerate called SABMiller. Six years later SABMiller entered a joint venture with Molson Coors to form MillerCoors. In yet another blockbuster deal, SABMiller became part of Anheuser-Busch InBev in 2016 but spun off its American holdings to Molson Coors to satisfy federal regulators. Miller has been a key player in a dizzying, high-stakes game of global beer poker, but its long story starts right here on Milwaukee's West Side.

Another world-class story begins on the exact same spot. A cabinetmaker named William Davidson and his family lived right here at Thirty-eighth and Highland, on what is now the corner of Miller's campus. In 1903 one of the Davidson sons, Arthur, and a friend named William Harley went to work in a ten-by-fifteen-foot shed in the family's backyard. Both young men were accomplished tinkerers, and their goal was to build a motorized bicycle that would outperform the competition. By 1904 they had completed four motorcycles in that legendary shed. The design evolved, manufacturing processes improved, and two more Davidson brothers joined the effort. By 1917 Harley-Davidson was turning out 18,000 motorcycles a year.

*Harley-Davidson began in this primitive shed behind the Davidson's family home on Highland Boulevard.*

### Turn right on 38th St.

They weren't made in that little shed, of course. The company expanded to new facilities across the street, and **Harley-Davidson** ❼ is still here. This is no longer a manufacturing facility, however. The engines are made in suburban Milwaukee and the bodies in York, Pennsylvania, but this complex has been corporate headquarters for decades, housing every division from IT to sales to engineering. In the post-pandemic world, the company has fully embraced remote work. Harley will remain an iconic presence on the West Side but, with fewer workers coming into the office, the main parking lot has been turned into a multi-purpose community park.

### Turn right on Juneau Ave.

The dominant theme in this section of the Near West Side is stability over the long term. One of the largest breweries in America and the heavyweight champion of motorcycles in the world are located directly across the street from each other, on sites that they have occupied from the very beginning. In Milwaukee or anywhere else, it would be hard to find a more powerful example of continuity in one place.

### Turn right on 35th St. and left on Highland Blvd.

# Concordia

You've completed the western leg of the tour. From here the route takes you back into the heart of the city, and the first neighborhood you see is Concordia. The name comes from a Missouri Synod Lutheran college that moved here in 1883. Concordia was a pre-seminary school for German-speaking Midwestern farm boys who planned to be ministers. Most were anything but wealthy, but their campus was soon surrounded by the homes of affluent Germans moving from central Milwaukee to what was then the equivalent of the suburbs. Highland Boulevard, in fact, rivaled Grand Avenue as the most prestigious address on the West Side.

## Pull over just before 3109 Highland.

Highland Boulevard still has a number of distinguished survivors. The so-called **Lion House ❶** at 3209 was built in 1897 for a downtown banker named George Koch. Even more impressive are the two **Pabst mansions ❷** across the street. The pillared pile on the left, at 3112, belonged to Fred Pabst, Jr. and its neighbor to the east, with the red tile roof, was the home of his brother Gustav. Their father, Fred, Sr., built his palatial home on Grand Avenue, and his sons built on Highland Boulevard, illustrating the westward movement of Milwaukee's upper crust. As you'd expect, both sons were executives at the family brewery. Notice the coach houses behind their homes. They are more elaborate than most single-family homes in the surrounding blocks, but they were basically garages, built to store the carriages and wagons of the Pabst families.

The brothers were next-door neighbors, and immediately west of Fred Jr's. home was the mansion of brewer Frederick Miller and his family; Aurora Family Service now occupies the site. Some of Highland's other patricians included the Gettelmans (brewing), Manegolds (milling), Vilters (manufacturing), and Usingers (sausage). There were so many well-heeled Germans on the street that Highland was once called "Sauerkraut Boulevard."

Just like their peers on Grand Avenue, the aristocrats of Highland began to move out when they felt mounting pressure for high-density development. In an exodus that lasted from the 1920s through the World War II years, they resettled in Milwaukee's western suburbs or on the city's East Side. When they departed, their lavish homes were either cut up into studio and efficiency units or torn down for new apartment construction, especially in the 1960s and '70s. The result was a remarkable increase in density. Mansions that once housed a single family and their servants might have been replaced by apartment buildings with 200 units.

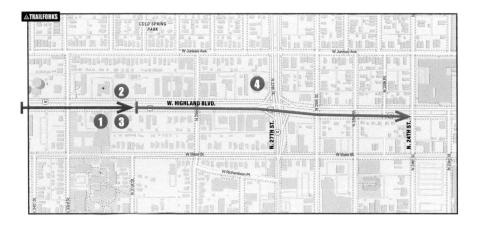

The homes in the interior of the neighborhood were also in harm's way. As real estate values declined in the 1960s, Concordia College went on a buying spree. The school had evolved from a pre-seminary institution to a four-year college with multiple specialties, and its leaders decided to expand in place. By 1980 the college owned more than 100 homes surrounding its original campus. Some were torn down for new facilities and others became rental units, but the college soon ran head-first into the preservation movement. Younger families, in particular, were attracted by the area's premium housing stock, and they put pressure on the school to take better care of its properties. Concordia, in a word, left. In 1983 the college moved to Mequon and started over in the former convent of the Notre Dame Sisters. Its residential properties were sold to the Westside Conservation Corporation, who rehabbed them for sale to owner-occupants.

The fate of the campus itself was an open question, but it eventually became the planned home of the Wisconsin Indian Cultural Center, a multi-program complex for the state's original residents. The center's leaders proposed high-stakes bingo as their primary source of funding, which elicited a strong reaction from the neighborhood's new homeowners. The tension was resolved when the Potawatomi tribe purchased land in the Menomonee Valley and opened America's first off-reservation casino there in 1991. The tribe has continued to transform the former Concordia campus. The fortress-like building behind the metal fence to your right is a Potawatomi-owned **data center,** ❸ a sort of electronic hotel for some of the most powerful computer arrays in the region.

### *Continue east to 27th St.*

As you continue east, Concordia's diversity shines through. Gracious old homes, including some reborn as bed-and-breakfasts, share the blocks with high-density apartment complexes and institutions like **St. Luke Emanuel Baptist Church,** ❹ a former Christian Science center. Few neighborhoods have so many stories to tell, and Concordia's story continues to the present day.

# Midtown

Twenty-seventh Street marks the entrance to the Midtown neighborhood, whose name has a double origin. You're near the middle of town, but these blocks were also the site of the Midtown Conservation Project, a 1970s urban renewal effort that was the first in Milwaukee to combine redevelopment with preservation. The result is a sometimes-jarring mixture of old and new, a contrast highly visible in the houses on both sides of Highland Boulevard. The north side of the street has a fine assortment of Milwaukee duplexes. Often associated with the German community, they reflect the typical immigrant's emphasis on thrift. The practice was to build a house that filled the entire lot, providing plenty of space for the owner's family downstairs and a tenant upstairs whose rent paid the monthly mortgage. The south side of Highland is lined with homes that are typically seventy years younger than the duplexes.

## Pause at 24th St.

On the left is **Milwaukee High School of the Arts,❶** also known as West Division. Milwaukee's public school system is often described in terms of its struggles, but MHSA is a real success story. Every student has a major in one of the visual or performing arts, and their work frequently approaches professional standards.

The Midtown project's dual emphasis—preservation and redevelopment—did create some problems. Disagreement about which houses to save and which to tear down led to protracted conflict between local residents and city officials. The wars are long forgotten, but the contrast between old and new remains startling.

## Turn left on 20th St.

That contrast is especially strong as you turn north on Twentieth Street. On the northwest corner is a **Schlitz mansion ❷** from 1890—built by a liquor wholesaler, not the beer baron—and on the right you see the Kilbourntown 3 project. "K3" represents urban renewal in its original form, which critics derided as "urban removal." The federally mandated policy was to level blighted neighborhoods and start over, regardless of the age or condition of individual houses.

## Turn right on McKinley Ave. and pull over at 19th St.

There is just one historic survivor in the Kilbourntown 3 project area, and it's a beauty. This is the **Robert Machek house,❸** built in 1894 by a Vienna-born woodcarver. Whether he intended it as an advertisement for his services or as a fill-in project between jobs, this home is hand-carved, both inside and out. Like all of its neighbors, it was slated for demolition, but a history-loving family purchased the house

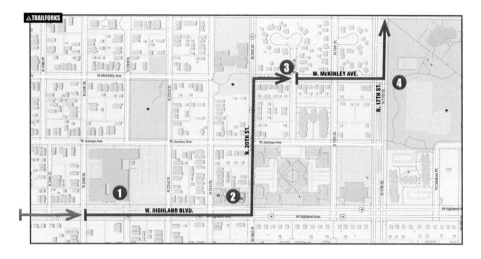

in 1964 and planned to restore it. "No exceptions," said the city, touching off a long battle with the owners. After an aggressive campaign to build support and attract publicity, the preservationists won. What you see here, many years later, is one of the most striking examples of the past in the present you will find in Milwaukee or anywhere else.

### Continue east on McKinley.

The rest of the area's homes are definitely suburban in style, again in conformity with federal redevelopment policies. If the average Milwaukeean were blindfolded, driven around town, and deposited in the Kilbourntown project, he or she might think they had landed in Germantown, Brown Deer, or Menomonee Falls—anywhere but the heart of the central city. This "suburb in the city" approach has been highly successful in promoting neighborhood stability, and it came with a twist in Milwaukee. As part of its New Hope initiative, the Housing Authority has scattered owner-occupied homes among its more numerous subsidized rental units. The goal is to encourage aspirations to homeownership among residents historically excluded from residential equity.

### Turn left on 17th St.

You are on the infinitely arguable border between the city's West and North Sides, but any historical signs of that division have long since been erased by redevelopment, most obviously **Martin Luther King Park**. **4** In the city's infancy, there was so much open land around Milwaukee that only a few visionaries suggested preserving any of it for parks. The result was a notable lack of open space in the central city. As part of the area's broader transformation in the late 1960s and early '70s, six square blocks of homes and businesses were cleared to create King Park. The green space was certainly welcome, but the displacement of scores of households was not.

*Turn right on Vliet St.*

Subsidized housing fills the blocks on the north side of Vliet Street, but soon you enter one of the North Side's historic retail hubs. Vliet was a typical streetcar-oriented shopping district that today is just a shadow of its former self. There are some wonderful murals here, but the only survivor from the street's heyday as a neighborhood "downtown" is the **old Schuster's store** ❺ on the north side at Eleventh. As I noted earlier, Schuster's grew to be the biggest department store chain in Wisconsin without a single downtown location. When Vliet Street's fortunes declined, this Schuster's was repurposed as a human services center, part of the Milwaukee County Department of Social Services.

### Turn left on 12th St. and pull over safely.

The historic **Pabst Brewing** ❻ complex dominates the landscape east of Interstate 43 and south of diagonal Winnebago Street. The brewery was launched on that hillside by the Best family in 1844, two years before Milwaukee became a city. Just three decades later, it was the largest producer in America. Phillip Best's flamboyant son-in-law, former lake captain Frederick Pabst, took over the business and renamed it for himself in 1889. Pabst had a secure place as one of the nation's three largest brewers for generations, alongside Schlitz and Anheuser-Busch, but it encountered increasing turbulence in the 1980s. Struggling with problems of succession, quality, and labor relations, the company was sold in 1985 to a California investor who bled it dry and closed the complex in 1996. For years it was a forlorn and forbidding hulk, with trees growing out of the rooftops, but in 2006 Joseph Zilber, a real estate mogul with roots in the neighborhood, purchased the brewery and turned it into a mixed-use development called, naturally, The Brewery. It has become a widely praised model of adaptive reuse whose occupants include a hotel, apartments, restaurants, offices, a film studio, and even a school of public health.

It seems fitting that a working brewery stands directly across the road north of the former Pabst brewery. **Leinenkugel** is a craft producer based in Chippewa Falls and owned by Miller Brewing. This highly automated facility produces some of "Leinie's" popular specialty brands, including seasonals like Honey Lemon Light.

### Continue north of Walnut St. and pull over safely.

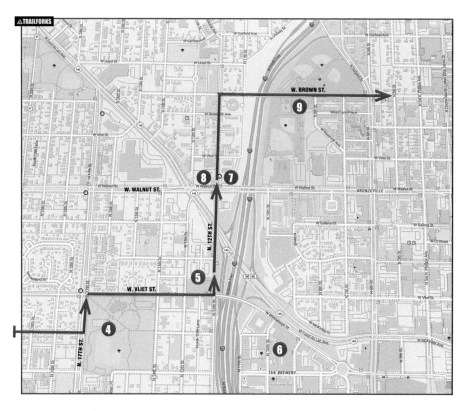

Walnut Street is the southern border of the Lindsay Heights neighborhood, a center of Black community life for decades, and here between two of its landmark institutions—**Speed Queen Bar-B-Q ❼** and **Mt. Sinai Community Baptist Church ❽**—is an appropriate place to briefly tell the story of Black Milwaukee. There have been African Americans here since 1835, when Joe Oliver, Solomon Juneau's cook, voted in Milwaukee's first election. By 1869 the community was large enough to support a church, and St. Mark's African Methodist Episcopal Church came to life on Fourth and Kilbourn. Growing slowly but steadily, Milwaukee's Black population approached 1000 in 1910 and then mushroomed with the start of the Great Migration. Legions of sharecroppers in the rural South became industrial workers in the urban North, and just over 7500 African Americans had settled in Milwaukee by 1930, most of them working in local industries. Chicago, however, was the more prominent destination in the upper Midwest, soaking up migrants like a giant sponge. Blacks made up seven percent of the Windy City's population in 1930 but just over one percent of Milwaukee's—a stark difference that lasted for decades. As late as 1970, in fact, Milwaukee's African-American community was proportionally the smallest of any in America's fifteen largest cities.

*Walnut Street was one of the Black community's major commercial corridors.*

*Home-grown institutions ranged from an accomplished choir at St. Mark African Methodist Episcopal Church ...*

*... to a top-notch baseball squad sponsored by the Milwaukee Urban League.*

That slow start had repercussions that still matter. In 1970, when Blacks made up 15 percent of the city's population, 54 percent of the metro area's Black males held production jobs in Milwaukee factories, compared with 23 percent of white males. They were finally earning union wages in a union town, putting homeownership, higher education, and second cars all within reach. Barely a decade later, a savage recession ripped through the industrial sector; Milwaukee lost one-fourth of its manufacturing jobs between 1979 and 1983. Deindustrialization pulled the rug out from under the city's emerging Black middle class, and the ratio of African Americans living in poverty spiked to 42 percent in 1990.

Redlining, restrictive housing covenants, and other weapons in the racist arsenal of the urban North had already limited Black residential choices to the older neighborhoods north of downtown. Deindustrialization intensified that pattern, first flattening the North Side's economy and then freezing it in place. As manufacturing jobs dried up, so did opportunities for mobility, and the result was a level of hypersegregation that has put Milwaukee in the same unhappy league as Chicago, Gary, Detroit, Cleveland, and Philadelphia. The Black community has shown enormous resilience over the years, but it is also the focal point of challenges that are all too common in America's cities.

## Turn right on Brown St.

As you pass over Interstate 43, notice the contrast between the busy six-lane superhighway below you and the neighborhood-serving streets you've been traveling. Freeways excel at moving traffic, but they're just as efficient at isolating us from the city around us.

**Beckum Park ❾** is one of the North Side's most historic open spaces. It was originally the site of the Schlitz beer garden, Milwaukee's largest. The garden's attractions ranged from diving horses to light opera, and an amphitheater on the grounds could accommodate 5000 people. Throngs of German families filled the garden on summer Sundays until the city began to develop an adequate system of public parks in the early 1900s; admission to them was free, and the beer you brought from home tasted just as good as the Schlitz in Schlitz Park. The advent of Prohibition in 1919 was the final blow. Some beer gardens were subdivided for homes, while others became public green spaces. Schlitz Park has had a number of names under public ownership: first Lapham, then Carver, and now Beckum, the home of a highly regarded Little League baseball program. The housing project on the right features a blend of owner-occupied and subsidized rental housing comparable to what you saw in Kilbourntown 3.

# Halyard Park

Crossing Sixth Street, you enter a different kind of park: a suburban-style subdivision named **Halyard Park ❶** in honor of Wilbur and Ardie Halyard, urban pioneers who founded the first financial institution in the Black community, Columbia Savings and Loan, in 1925. This was originally an architecturally eclectic German neighborhood, but it became a specimen of urban blight in the years following World War II. Scores of homes were demolished for an urban renewal program in the 1970s, but funding was suspended before clearance was complete, creating a landscape that one resident described as "a mouth with half the teeth knocked out." A coalition of Black-owned real estate firms who had banded together as United Realty saw an opportunity. They approached the city and said, "If you complete acquiring and clearing these blighted homes, we'll put up a conventional subdivision," which is exactly what happened. In sharp contrast to some of the careworn neighborhoods nearby, Halyard Park is an upper middle-income development, full of three-bedroom homes with generous yards and fireplaces in the family rooms; one even has an indoor swimming pool.

By law, the neighborhood is open to everyone, but it happens to be a haven for the Black middle class. Residents appreciate the quality of the housing and the convenience of their location, but choosing Halyard Park is also an act of faith in the city's North Side. The district is often portrayed in the media as poverty-stricken and crime-ridden, but this, too, is the North Side—an object lesson in the importance of looking beyond stereotypes. On the strength of its success here, United Realty has developed other suburban-style projects in the heart of town.

The Romanesque landmark on the right is **St. Francis Church.❷** It was built in 1876 to serve the area's German Catholics, but today's congregation is remarkably diverse, with sizable concentrations of Puerto Ricans and African Americans.

## Turn left on Vel Phillips Ave.

N. Fourth Street was renamed Vel Phillips Avenue in 2018 to honor the first African American (and first woman) to serve on Milwaukee's Common Council. The civil rights trailblazer was also the first Black candidate and first woman to win statewide elective office when she became Wisconsin's secretary of state in 1978.

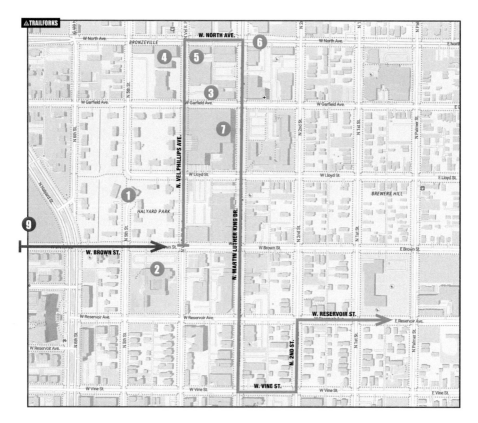

*The Halyard Park project is an inner-city development with a strongly suburban character.*

At Garfield Avenue you enter **Bronzeville,** ❸ an old name for a district brimming with new life. In the early decades of the twentieth century, Bronzeville was the Black community's center for entertainment, dotted with clubs that featured national per-formers like Duke Ellington and Louis Armstrong. In recent years the area has developed a critical mass of institutions that make it a center of community gravity in the twenty-first century. The new Bronzeville's anchors include the **American Black Holocaust Museum** ❹ (401 W. North Ave.), founded in 1988 by Dr. James Cameron, the survivor of a lynching attempt in Indiana; the **Milwaukee Urban League** ❺ (435 W. North Ave.), an essential resource for education, employment, and community advocacy since 1919; and newer attractions that range from art galleries to restaurants.

### *Turn right on North Ave. and right again on Martin Luther King Dr.*

The intersection of **North Avenue and King Drive** ❻ (formerly N. Third St.) is one of the most historic crossings on the North Side. It was the heart of the Third Street shopping district when Third was the German community's downtown, with retail sales volume second only to Wisconsin Avenue's. The street was so German that stories survive of merchants placing signs in their windows promising "English Spoken Here" to avoid scaring away the occasional non-Teutonic customer. The district is still a showcase for some of the city's finest Victorian commercial architec-ture, especially visible on the upper stories.

Third and North was also the epicenter of the 1967 riot, when Milwaukee became one of more than 100 US cities to experience racial violence during that long, hot summer. Retailers left in droves after the disturbance, and Third became a commer-cial ghost town. With help from city government and private enterprise, King Drive, a name adopted in 1984, began a spirited revival in the Eighties, and its renaissance continues. One of the most impressive projects is **ThriveOn King** ❼ (2153 King Drive), a novel collaboration that includes offices for the Greater Milwaukee Founda-tion and the Medical College of Wisconsin, mixed-income residential units, and amenities for healthy living. The effort has completely transformed the former flagship of the Schuster's department store chain, turning a historic commercial anchor into a modern community anchor.

### *Turn left on Vine St., left again on 2nd St., and right on Reservoir Ave.*

The Schuster Dry Goods Co., Third Street and Garfield Avenue, Milwaukee, Wis.

*Third Street was the North Side's busiest retail district for many years, and its anchor was Schuster's Department Store.*

*Renamed for Dr. Martin Luther King in 1984, the street hosts one of America's largest Juneteenth Day celebrations, commemorating the end of slavery.*

# Brewer's Hill

Between King Drive and the Milwaukee River lies Brewer's Hill, one of the oldest neighborhoods in Milwaukee. Development here began in the 1850s, and the first residents were predominantly German. Although they spoke a common language, their economic circumstances differed wildly. Milwaukee was a walking city in its early years. Everyone had to live close to everything, which meant that people who owned factories and people who swept factories were sometimes next-door neighbors in Brewer's Hill. That democratic pattern is clearly preserved in today's landscape.

Known for much of its history as simply the Sixth Ward, the neighborhood scraped bottom in the 1960s. Dozens of vintage homes fell to the wrecking ball, and the rest seemed likely to meet the same fate. Fortunately, first-wave preservationists began to discover the community in the mid-1970s. Arriving one step ahead of the wreckers, they purchased fine old homes for perhaps $10,000 and proceeded to spend major multiples of that amount restoring them. The movement developed such irresistible momentum that new homes, including those from 132 to 114 W. Reservoir, were built in the same styles as the originals, and the former **Weyenberg shoe factory,** ❶ ahead of you on the left, was converted to condominiums. If you had told any Milwaukeean in the 1970s that people would one day pay $250,000 for one-bedroom units in an old North Side shoe factory, the likely response would have been laughter, but that is precisely what happened.

## Turn right on Palmer St.

Brewer's Hill is a Lazarus neighborhood, a community that rose from the dead, and the 1800 block of Palmer St. showcases both new life and the original pattern of economic diversity. The mansion at **1823 N. Palmer** ❷ was for many years the home of Joseph Phillips, a tannery owner and prominent Democrat with epically bad political judgment. Phillips served one term as Milwaukee's mayor, from 1870 to 1871, but was buried in his bid for a second after he proposed closing the city's dance halls on Sunday. That was the equivalent of political suicide. The Phillips home was among the first to be rescued by preservationists in the mid-1970s, and it has since been surrounded by a lush and meticulously tended garden that is regularly open to the public.

Notice the cottage across the street at 1810 Palmer. It's so small that you could fit four or five of them inside the Phillips mansion, but that's one of Brewer's Hill's hallmarks: castles and cottages on the same blocks.

South of Vine Street, you can see why preservationists gave the neighborhood its present name in the 1970s: it's on a hillside overlooking the Schlitz brewery. Schlitz was founded in 1849 and moved to this riverside location in 1870. It was perennially a runner-up to Pabst in the national rankings, but in 1902 "the beer that made Milwaukee famous" became the best-selling brew in America. Schlitz prospered until

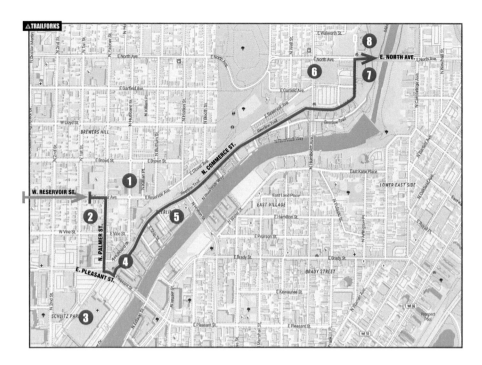

the 1970s, when a combination of succession issues, labor conflict, and self-inflicted quality problems triggered its sale to much-smaller Stroh's of Detroit in 1982. Stroh's closed the plant, causing significant anguish in a city with such a proud brewing heritage. Local capitalists redeveloped the complex as **Schlitz Park**, ❸ a mixed-use office park that now employs more people than the brewery in its heyday. One of the project's more unusual tenants is a public school for the gifted and talented named for the neighborhood's most famous former resident: Golda Meir.

## *Turn left on Pleasant St. and left again on Commerce St.*

**Commerce Street** ❹ is another conspicuous success story, with a history even longer than Brewer's Hill's. It began as the first leg of a canal envisioned by Byron Kilbourn as a link between his West Side settlement and the Gulf of Mexico via the Rock, Illinois, and Mississippi Rivers. Kilbourn made enemies as easily as Milwaukee's other founders made friends, and Wisconsin's legislature scuttled the project when he had completed little more than a mile. No problem. Kilbourn turned his snippet of canal into a millrace fed by water impounded behind a dam near North Avenue. That millrace became Milwaukee's first industrial district, supporting flour mills, tanneries, and a variety of other businesses. Steam engines eventually replaced "the water power," and Kilbourn's ditch was filled in and paved over in 1885 to become Commerce Street. Today's residents probably have no idea that their home address was once a historic waterway.

One by one, Commerce Street's factories closed or moved away over the years, and the street became an industrial wasteland after World War II, a corridor of coal piles that gave East Siders a sooty shortcut to downtown. With a major boost from city officials, Commerce Street became a development opportunity after 2000. It now features some of the finest, and priciest, multi-family housing in the city; chrome and glass have replaced coal and garbage. The transformation has been so rapid that Milwaukeeans who haven't driven down Commerce recently can barely recognize the place.

One important business is still located on Commerce Street: the **Lakefront Brewery.** ❺ Despite its name, the company has been here on the Milwaukee River since 1998. Lakefront is a leader among Milwaukee's craft breweries, and its tour is one of the best; the guides are entertaining, the pours are generous, and you can keep the glass. A cavernous restaurant occupies the upper floor of this former power plant, and Friday night fish fries feature oompah bands in the best Milwaukee tradition. The Holton Street viaduct practically overshadows the brewery, and the "marsupial" bridge suspended in its framework offers bikers and pedestrians a novel way to travel between the East and North Sides.

Before we leave the riverfront, try to recall the range of neighborhoods you've experienced in the last fifteen minutes or so: the Black suburban-style homes of

*A millrace that powered Milwaukee's pioneer industrial district in the 1850s ...*

Halyard Park, the cultural buzz of Bronzeville, the Victorian storefronts of King Drive, the castles and cottages of Brewer's Hill, and the cutting-edge condos of Commerce Street. Together these contrasting communities cover no more than a square mile, demonstrating one of the things I love most about cities: the multitude of worlds they contain in just a handful of square blocks. Only in large cities will you find such striking diversity on such a small scale.

## *Cross Humboldt Ave.*

You're on the southern edge of **Riverwest**, ⑥ a neighborhood that over the last 150 years has provided homes for working-class Poles, Italians from the Brady Street area, Puerto Ricans from the edge of downtown, Blacks from the North Side, and countercultural refugees from the East Side. They're all still here, in varying proportions, making Riverwest one of the most diverse and most welcoming neighborhoods in Milwaukee.

The north end of Commerce Street continues the pattern of high-end multi-family housing so visible farther south, and one development hints at the prevailing demographic. Residents of the **Belay Apartments** ⑦ (2200 Commerce) share their building with Adventure Rock, a climbing gym to which they automatically belong. Senior housing this is not. Directly across North Avenue is another youth-oriented development: **RiverView Hall**, ⑧ a UW-Milwaukee dormitory connected by frequent shuttle service with the main campus on the East Side.

*… was filled in to become Commerce Street in 1885.*

MILWAUKEE COUNTY HISTORICAL SOCIETY

*Rohn's swimming school drew a motley crew of water enthusiasts to the Milwaukee River.*

*"Water bicycles" plied the upper river as thrill-seekers zipped down Shoot the Chutes in the background.*

*The river was a year-round attraction, thronged with skaters as soon as the ice was thick enough.*

### Turn right on North Ave. and pull over safely at the approach to the bridge. ❾

You're about to cross one of the most important stretches of Milwaukee's most important river. Downstream to the right is a pedestrian bridge that marks the site of a dam that was removed in 1997. The first incarnation of that barrier powered the city's pioneer industrial district, but it also created a long, narrow lake that extended nearly two miles upstream. During the long years of one-day weekends and no air conditioning for our ancestors, there was a desperate need for recreational opportunities close to home during the hot summer months. The upper river filled the bill. From the 1870s to the 1920s, it was lined with a rotating assortment of swimming schools, canoe clubs, beer gardens, amusement parks, and other attractions that made it a sort of in-town Up North. There was even a water toboggan ride called Shoot the Chutes that sent thrill-seekers hurtling down the bluff on the east side of this bridge. Long before Wisconsin Dells claimed the title, the upper river was a waterpark in its own right.

By the 1930s, pollution and competition from other venues had ended the river's glory days, and it became a desolate, degraded urban waterway for the next sixty years. The removal of the North Avenue dam, coupled with ongoing improvements in water quality, began a promising new chapter in the stream's long history. The mudflats that emerged in the 1990s were reclaimed by nature to become the focus of a public-private partnership whose leaders saw the upper river as a new kind of in-town Up North. The result was the Milwaukee River Greenway, an urban wilderness that covers 900 acres and six miles of shoreline, with hiking and biking trails, canoe launches, and an arboretum filled with native plants. Starting barely a mile from City Hall, the Greenway is a priceless environmental corridor that is exceedingly rare, perhaps even unique, in urban America.

### Cross the river and continue to Oakland Ave.

# Upper East Side

The East Side is by far the smallest of Milwaukee's major districts. Only a mile wide and four miles long, it occupies just four percent of the city's land area, but this undersized area plays an outsized role in the life of the larger community. As a center of tastes and a setter of trends, the East Side stands alone. The district's influence is a consequence of several things, including high population densities, a heavy concentration of young adults, and the cosmopolitan mix of students and faculty associated with the University of Wisconsin-Milwaukee.

But the East Side had a robust identity decades before UWM existed. From the 1870s through the 1920s, settlement here followed two contrasting corridors: wealthy near the lake and working-class near the river. Those contrasts persist in the landscape of today, making the East Side an intriguing collection of distinct but overlapping worlds.

Just past Bartlett Avenue on the left, you can glimpse a popular East Side amenity directly below you: the **Oak Leaf bike trail.** ❶ Once a busy North Western Railroad line, the paved path traverses the entire East Side without a single stop signal and connects to other rail trails that continue into Sheboygan County.

## Turn left on Oakland Ave.

North Avenue is lined with restaurants, nightspots, and other East Side specialties, but Oakland Avenue is more thoroughly residential. This is the west side of the East Side, the working-class corridor, and it's lined with relatively modest frame homes, duplexes, and small apartment buildings. But Oakland is also the home of the **Shambhala Meditation Center** ❷ at 2344, an East Side mainstay that reflects the district's characteristic embrace of cultural alternatives.

At Riverside Place you glimpse a corner of **Riverside Park,** ❸ acquired in 1890 and developed as one of the city's first major green spaces. Riverside's best-known amenity is the Urban Ecology Center, an internationally recognized outdoor education program that uses the park as a classroom. The UEC's admirably green building is in the southwest corner (at 1500 E. Park Place) and open to all if you want to take a break.

## Turn right on Newberry Blvd.

Newberry Boulevard is a green link between Riverside and Lake Parks, but it also resembles a geological formation, encapsulating the history of the larger district in wood and brick. A definite economic gradient is apparent as you travel from west to east. The homes near Oakland Avenue are certainly comfortable, as you'd expect on a leafy boulevard, but most are of frame construction and many are duplexes.

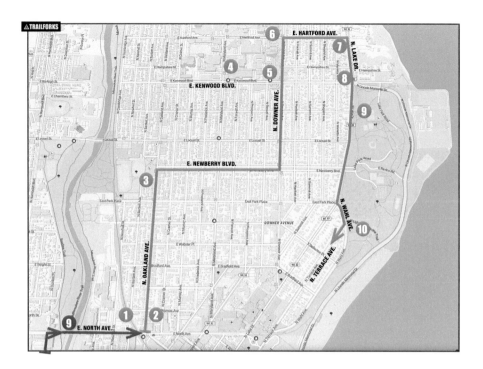

As you head east, the houses become larger and more distinctive, stone and brick replace wooden siding, and duplexes give way to single-family homes. The standout at 2430 was designed by Russell Barr Williamson, who, as you might have guessed, was an associate of Frank Lloyd Wright.

## *Turn left on Downer Ave.*

You begin to feel the presence of **UW-Milwaukee** ❹ as you travel north on Downer Avenue. The university opened in 1956 and quickly became the second-largest school in the state system, trailing only UW-Madison. With 23,000 students (2023 enrollment) and an extensive research program, UWM is an educational engine for the entire state; most of its students are Wisconsinites who stay in Wisconsin after graduation. The school's impact on the immediate neighborhood is even more profound; UWM is a major influence on the East Side's culture, its housing market, and its parking.

Crossing Kenwood Boulevard, the first campus building you see on the left is **Mitchell Hall**, ❺ which plays the role of Old Main for UWM. It opened in 1909 as the Milwaukee State Normal School, a teacher's college, and now anchors an educational complex that sprawls across more than 100 acres.

MILWAUKEE JOURNAL SENTINEL

*The University of Wisconsin-Milwaukee, shown here in 1981, has had a profound impact on both the city and its East Side neighborhood.*

The graceful red brick buildings in the next block formed the campus of **Milwaukee-Downer College**, 6 a pioneering women's institution that moved to this location in 1899. The entire Milwaukee-Downer ensemble was absorbed by UWM in 1964.

## *Turn right on Hartford Ave.*

The Kenwood Park neighborhood is an upper-middle-income community whose incomes become less middle and more upper as you near Lake Drive, an address that has long been synonymous with wealth in Milwaukee. Here you enter the stratosphere of city housing. The mansion on the corner of Lake and Marietta was built in 1913 for industrialist Armin Schlesinger; it is now UWM's **Hefter Conference Center.** 7

## *Turn right on Lake Dr.*

Homes designed by architects for affluent families line both sides of Lake Drive, and those on the left are perched atop a bluff that descends all the way to the shore of Lake Michigan. Some of the largest homes have been replaced by new but still opulent dwellings, and a few have been converted to other uses. The mansion at the corner of Lake and Kenwood was built for lawyer Horace Upham in 1912. It is now the **Lubavitch House,** 8 the Wisconsin center of a worldwide movement to reinvigorate traditional Judaism.

Crossing Kenwood Boulevard again, **Lake Park** 9 is on your left. One of Milwaukee's most notable and least celebrated achievements has been preserving its shoreline for public use. More than half of the county's lakefront is in the public domain, and parks are strung like pearls on a necklace from Fox Point to South Milwaukee.

*The North Point lighthouse in Lake Park is a scenic highlight in one of Milwaukee's most scenic open spaces.*

Lake Park is arguably the most lustrous pearl. Acquired in 1890, it was designed by the firm of Frederick Law Olmsted, the most prominent landscape architect in American history; his other projects included Central Park in New York City. Olmsted's crews developed elegant carriageways and wooded walking trails that make it hard to believe you're near the heart of a major city. They also filled in a deep ravine to create a great meadow, which is now a par-three golf course. A much older park amenity is one of the few remaining Indian mounds in Milwaukee, the low-rise knoll visible near the bus turn-around at the foot of Locust Street.

### *Turn left on Wahl Ave.*

One of the gems in the East Side's landscape is the **North Point Lighthouse** ⓾ on the left. The light was decommissioned in 1994, but the keeper's residence has been converted to a fine small museum. You can top off your visit by climbing the lighthouse tower for a gorgeous view of Lake Michigan and downtown Milwaukee.

### *Turn right on Terrace Ave.*

# North Point

Terrace Avenue continues the theme of affluent residential development on the east side of the East Side. The stone mansion on the right, at 2675, was built in 1931 for the family of Alfred Slocum. The Slocums owned a thriving straw hat factory, but Alfred had also married A.O. Smith's daughter, Gertrude, which may have helped with the down payment.

On the far end of the block, at 2611 Terrace, is a scaled-down German castle built for the family of tanner Gustav Trostel, whose leather factory was one of the largest businesses on Commerce Street. When it was completed in 1900 (thirty-one years before the Slocum home), this mansion was beyond the leading edge of settlement on the East Side; the Trostels' friends reportedly chided them for moving so far out into the country.

On the opposite side of Terrace in the next block, at 2506, is the boyhood home of Edmund Fitzgerald. Although he was descended from a line of ship captains and shipbuilders, Fitzgerald made his mark as president of Northwestern Mutual Life, a position he held from 1947 to 1958. In 1956, seeking greater diversity in its investments, NML built the largest object ever to hit fresh water: an iron ore carrier that the company's trustees named for their leader. The *Edmund Fitzgerald* set multiple tonnage records over the years, but the ship's enduring fame was posthumous. In 1975 it went down in "the gales of November," one of the worst tragedies in the modern history of the Great Lakes. That was notoriety enough, but then Gordon Lightfoot released *The Wreck of the Edmund Fitzgerald*. The song became a classic, making Edmund Fitzgerald the only insurance executive in world history whose name became a household word.

Farther south on Terrace, at 2420, is the **Frederick Bogk home,** ❶ designed, as you might have guessed, by Frank Lloyd Wright. He was a native son of Wisconsin, born in Richland Center in 1867. Wright's early practice was centered in Chicago and its western suburbs, particularly Oak Park and River Forest, but he had a number of Wisconsin commissions. This home, built for a prominent businessman's family in 1917, has typical Prairie Style elements—generous eaves, slot windows, strong horizontal lines—but it was designed during the time Wright was working on the Imperial Hotel in Tokyo. It's not too hard to see a Japanese teahouse here. This is one Wright home that's been lovingly maintained from the beginning, and it remains a great example of the master's craft.

*Pause at North Ave., then continue on Terrace Ave.*

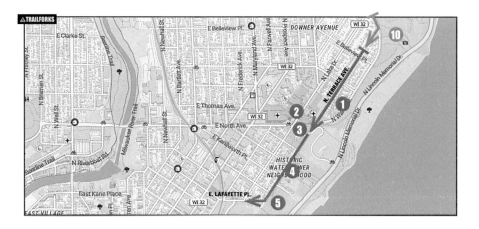

North Avenue is the midpoint of the North Point neighborhood. It offers a gorgeous view of Lake Michigan that shows clearly the deep indentation of Milwaukee Bay. The street also marks the city's northern limits when Milwaukee incorporated in 1846. One of the first buildings here was St. Mary's Hospital, which evolved into the **Ascension Columbia St. Mary's ❷** health care complex on the right. St. Mary's was the first public hospital in Wisconsin; it began downtown in 1848 and relocated here a decade later, after city officials decided that this "seat of pestilence" would be better located on the edge of town.

The area's dominant landmark has long been the **North Point Water Tower.❸** When Milwaukee developed its first municipal water system in the early 1870s, the pumps at the foot of the bluff were like gigantic mechanical hearts, bringing lake water up the hill in pulses. The extreme variations in pressure threatened the water main, and so the city installed a standpipe at the top of the bluff to absorb the surges and let the water back into the main gradually. The purely utilitarian wrought iron pipe was encased in a fairy-tale castle that resembles something out of the Brothers Grimm—Rapunzel comes to mind—and it's been North Point's trademark ever since.

A row of particularly distinguished homes overlooks the lake south of Water Tower Park. The first, at 2236 Terrace, was built in 1895 for the family of William Goodrich, a linseed oil manufacturer whose wife happened to be Marie Pabst. Her father, beer baron Frederick Pabst, reportedly gave this home to the couple as a wedding present, and it does bear at least some resemblance to a wedding cake.

Next door, at 2230, is a limestone mansion built for the family of Marie's brother, Gustav Pabst, who moved here in 1907 from the Highland Boulevard home you saw back in the Concordia neighborhood. It's intriguing to imagine Marie and Gus trading family gossip over the backyard fence.

The next house south, at 2220, is the real standout in this procession of fine homes. Built in 1924, **Villa Terrace** ❹ was the home of Lloyd Raymond Smith, who succeeded his father, A.O. Smith, as head of the largest manufacturer of automobile and truck frames in the world. The Smiths hired David Adler, a well-known society architect, to design what is basically a Mediterranean villa. True to the source of their inspiration, they called their home "Sopra Mare"—"above the sea" in Italian. (My Italian friends point out that it should really be 'Sopra Lago—"above the lake.") The number "410" on the gateposts is a rare remnant of Milwaukee's old street numbering system. Villa Terrace survives because Ray Smith's widow, Agnes, donated it to the people of Milwaukee in 1966. It's now a museum of the decorative arts and a popular venue for weddings, concerts, and other gatherings. One of the mansion's most appealing features is a formal garden that cascades down the bluff all the way to the lakefront.

The neighboring home, at 2214, was the residence of Herman Falk and his wife, Eva, for nearly fifty years. Falk owned one of the largest manufacturers of precision industrial gears in the world. Now a division of Regal Rexnord, the Falk gear plant still operates in its original location in the Menomonee Valley.

**Back Bay Park,** ❺ in the next block, is a quiet corner of green space in the North Point neighborhood. Sometimes called Baby Park for its diminutive size, Back Bay is the baby brother of Lake Park. As unimaginable as it may seem today, the park was once covered with houses of the same size and vintage as the fine homes around it. They were cleared in the early decades of the twentieth century, long before the preservation movement took hold, reflecting the governing Socialists' belief that the best views belong to all the people, not just the wealthy few. The park is an ambiguous amenity that is somehow laudable and horrifying at the same time.

### Turn right on Lafayette Pl. and left down Lafayette Hill Rd.

Descending to the lakefront, the first landmark you see on the right is **Colectivo Coffee,** ❻ a fine Cream City brick structure with a disgusting past. In 1888, long after Milwaukee had turned its principal river into an open sewer, the city decided to "solve" the problem by digging a tunnel under the East Side, installing the world's largest water pump in this building, and using the fresh lake water to flush the putrid Milwaukee River. It was actually called the "flushing station." The river got cleaner, but where did all that filth go? The lake. And where did Milwaukee get its drinking water? The lake. Whenever the sewage plume drifted over the water intake, cases of typhoid fever would spike ominously—a supposedly Third World health problem that was killing people throughout urban America. It was not until 1925, when Milwaukee began to actually treat its sewage in a state-of-the-art plant on Jones Island, that the "river nuisance" was effectively abated.

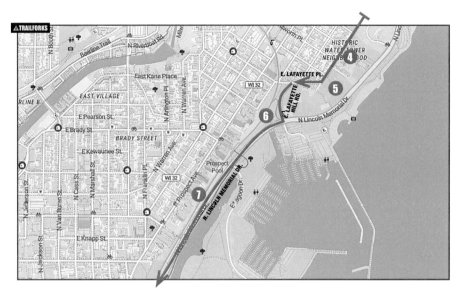

*The seam between the Juneau Park lagoon and the North Western railroad tracks became Lincoln Memorial Drive in the 1920s.*

## Turn right on Lincoln Memorial Dr.

You would have been underwater at this point 150 years ago. Lincoln Memorial Drive consists entirely of landfill deposited here over many decades for two reasons: erosion control and parkland. When the drive was completed in 1929, it became perhaps the most cherished green space in Milwaukee, and it's still one of the finest stretches of urban shoreline on the Great Lakes. The idea was to protect the shore and at the same time open Milwaukee's greatest natural resource to everyone, a decidedly Socialist concept. Lincoln Memorial is still the city's pride, and any attempts to alter it are met with fierce resistance.

The **Oak Leaf bicycle trail** ❼ is visible behind the shrubbery on the right. It occupies the former right-of-way of the Chicago & North Western Railroad, whose tracks were once so close to the water that storm waves would occasionally wash them away.

*Turn left at the entrance to the Milwaukee Art Museum and follow the drive around to the right.*

Passing under the Mason Street bridge, you're directly below the tour's starting point and in the immediate presence of two iconic buildings. I've always viewed the War Memorial Center and the **Art Museum addition** ❽ as two birds perched on the lakefront: the blocky 1957 creation of Eero Saarinen and the lighter, almost ethereal 2001 composition of Santiago Calatrava. This powerful pairing of modernist and futurist design is unique in Milwaukee and far beyond. "The Calatrava," as it's called, has become a particular point of local pride. It's not just a place to showcase art but a work of art in itself, a kinetic sculpture whose wings open and close with all the grace of a colossal swan. If Milwaukee had its own postage stamp, the Calatrava would be on it.

### *Continue to first stop sign and turn right onto Michigan St.*

The Cudahy Gardens, designed by Dan Kiley, serve as an elegant green threshold for the Art Museum addition, with a water feature active in season. **Discovery World,** ❾ on the lakefront to the left, is a fascinating hybrid of a water-centric museum, complete with fresh- and salt-water aquariums, and a hands-on science and technology center, targeted particularly to young people. The entire downtown lakefront has been transformed since 2000, becoming a cultural theme park that is among the city's top tourist destinations. Overlooking it all from the other side of Lincoln Memorial Drive is the **Couture,** ❿ a high-end, high-rise apartment tower. At forty-four stories, the Couture is the tallest residential building in the state.

*Turn left at light to re-enter Lincoln Memorial Dr. Stay left and follow the Lincoln Memorial Dr. signs carefully to avoid entering the freeway.*

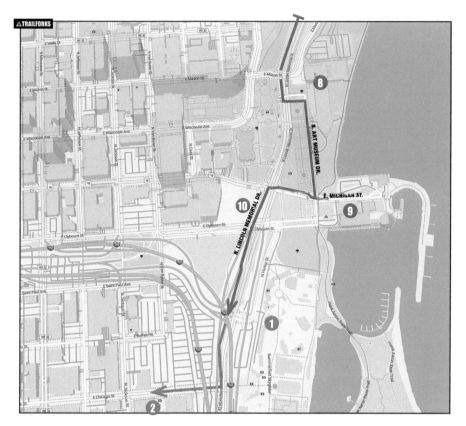

*Landfill activity has been a lakefront constant. This 1957 addition now supports the American Family Amphitheater at Maier Festival Park.*

# Third Ward

As you thread your way through the concrete spaghetti at the approach to the Dan Hoan Bridge, **Maier Festival Park** ❶ is on your left. Named for Henry Maier, Milwaukee's longest-serving mayor (1960-1988), the site has had multiple incarnations. Beginning as lakebed, it became a freightyard in the 1870s, a downtown airport in 1927, a Nike anti-aircraft missile base in 1956, and the permanent home of Summerfest in 1970. Promoted as the world's largest music festival, Summerfest showcases some 800 bands that draw hundreds of thousands of fans to the lakefront every summer. (Peak attendance was just over one million in 2001.) Although baby boomers are no longer its target demographic, I attend Summerfest regularly. If you can't find something to like with so much to choose from, you're simply being too picky.

Although Summerfest is the main event, the park is busy throughout the summer. The lineup starts with Pridefest in June, a celebration of LGBTQ+ culture, and then shifts to ethnic gatherings: Polish Fest, German Fest, Black Arts Fest, Irish Fest, and Mexican Fiesta. Irish Fest is the largest of the lot; come rain or shine, it attracts at least 100,000 patrons every year, making it the largest celebration of Irish culture and music on the planet.

## Turn right at first stop sign onto Chicago St.

Leaving the deep shade of the Hoan Bridge, you enter the heart of the storied Third Ward. The **Italian Community Center** ❷ is the major landmark, but this is a community with multiple historic layers. It began as a native wetland that was filled in to become Milwaukee's pioneer Irish neighborhood. Known as the "Bloody Third," the district had the highest concentration of saloons (and the highest arrest rate) in the city, but it provided easy access to employment on the docks, the railroads, and in Milwaukee's first industries. A disastrous 1892 fire left 2500 Third Warders homeless, accelerating the Irish community's migration to the Tory Hill and Merrill Park neighborhoods you visited on the West Side.

As the Irish moved out, Italians moved in; one ghetto succeeded another. Overwhelmingly Sicilian, the newcomers took the same blue-collar jobs as their predecessors, but a significant number went into the produce business, making the Third Ward Milwaukee's primary source of fresh fruits and vegetables. As the immigrants' children prospered, they moved out, most often to the Lower East Side, leaving their aging parents behind in rapidly aging houses. Blight became so prevalent that the Third Ward had the dubious distinction of being chosen for Milwaukee's first urban renewal project. In 1955, despite stubborn resistance from long-time residents, the heart of the community was leveled. The crowning blow came in 1967, when the community's place of worship, Our Lady of Pompeii Church, was torn down to make way for Interstate 794.

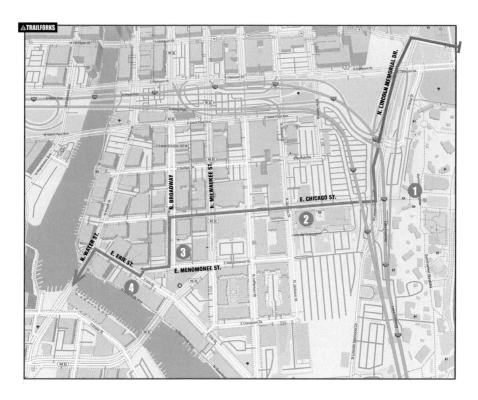

*Our Lady of Pompeii Church served the Third Ward's Sicilians.*

*Summerfest serves music-lovers from throughout the region. The grounds were largely undeveloped in this 1976 view.*

*Just blocks from the open horizon of Lake Michigan, the Third Ward was one of Milwaukee's most densely settled immigrant neighborhoods.*

*Broadway's Commission Row was the center of the city's wholesale fruit and vegetable business.*

Emotional ties to the old neighborhood remained strong despite the demolition. In 1978 a loyal core of former Lady of Pompeii parishioners decided to hold a reunion on the Summerfest grounds and invite the public. The result was Festa Italiana, the first and for many years the largest of Milwaukee's lakefront ethnic celebrations. Proceeds from Festa made it possible to build the **Italian Community Center** in 1990. It was a literal homecoming, and Festa Italiana is now held as an old-fashioned street festival on the ICC's grounds.

### *Cross Milwaukee St. and turn left on Broadway.*

Milwaukee Street is a razor-sharp dividing line between the redeveloped urban renewal area behind you and the neighborhood as it looked in the early 1900s: a conglomeration of multi-story brick warehouses and light manufacturing plants built after the 1892 fire. These monumental buildings were practically obsolete by the 1950s, hampered by inefficient layouts and inadequate truck access. One by one they were shuttered, and the neighborhood felt increasingly like a ghost town. But together they offered Wisconsin's largest concentration of exposed beams and open brick walls—prized amenities as the preservation movement took off in the 1970s. Drawn by the district's architecture as well as its proximity to downtown, developers flocked to the Third Ward, sparking a renaissance that continues to the present. Old knitwear plants were reborn as pricey new condos, and street-level spaces came alive with restaurants, galleries, specialty shops, nightspots, and cultural attractions like the **Broadway Theater Center.** ❸  The Third Ward's population soared from 74 in 1980 to nearly 3000 in the mid-2020s, reflecting the worn-out industrial district's transformation into one of the most fashionable addresses in the city.

### *Turn right on Menomonee St. and right again on Erie St.*

The **Milwaukee Institute of Art and Design** ❹ is a fitting symbol of the Third Ward's continuing rebirth. It was built in 1920 as the Terminal Building, a sort of industrial condominium that housed dozens of entrepreneurs intent on turning their small businesses into large ones. In 1992 the building became the home of MIAD, Wisconsin's only private four-year college of art and design.

### *Turn left on Water St. and cross the Milwaukee River bridge.*

# Walker's Point

The stand-alone brick structure on the right side of the bridge at 105 N. Water, now a residence, was built as the city's fireboat station in 1915, when blazes in riverfront buildings were all too common. As you cross the river, look downstream for a panoramic view of what I call **Condo Canyon,** ❶ a trendy blend of new construction and repurposed industrial buildings. Upstream, at the railroad swing bridge, the Menomonee River dies continuously into the Milwaukee.

### Pull over at the south end of the bridge.

Walker's Point is without question the oldest neighborhood in Milwaukee. Its pioneer rivals, Juneautown and Kilbourntown, have long since vanished under layers of downtown development, but the South Side's founding settlement is still relatively intact. It began in 1834, when George Walker, a native of Virginia, built his cabin at the tip of a narrow peninsula extending into the Milwaukee River very close to where you've paused. Given its proximity to the city's front door—the river mouth— Walker's modest point probably should have become the nucleus of Milwaukee's downtown, but the founder had multiple handicaps: a shortage of both cash and political clout, a clouded title, and his own laid-back personality. Described by one contemporary as "a free liver," Walker obviously had a hearty appetite; he weighed 350 pounds long before Doritos and Twinkies arrived on the culinary scene. Despite his girth, the original South Sider was said to be the finest ice skater in Wisconsin Territory, with the qualifier "when the ice was thick enough."

George Walker's slow start had long-term repercussions. His settlement was by far the smallest of the three that united to form the city in 1846, and that pattern endured. To this day, even though they're of equal size, the north half of Milwaukee County has two residents for every one in the south half, which is why Franklin and Oak Creek still have farms and the northern reaches of the county are completely developed. Once again, history is why things are the way they are. The silver lining was that the south side of the Menomonee Valley experienced far less development pressure than the north, and less pressure meant less demolition; a significant number of early buildings survive to the present, making Walker's Point a showcase for historic preservation.

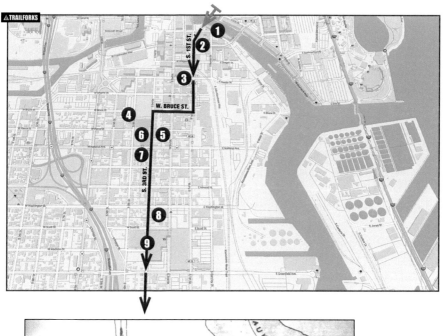

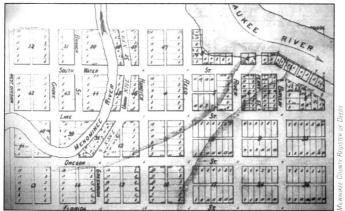

*George Walker settled at the tip of an actual point in 1834.*
*It ended at the site of today's Water Street bridge.*

## Continue on S.1st St. and pull over at Florida St.

Much like its neighboring community across the river, Walker's Point has experienced a transformation in recent years. New buildings have gone up, and old industrial structures have been repurposed as artist's lofts, apartments, offices, and shops. **Colectivo Coffee,** ❷ 170 S. First, is a good example of adaptive reuse; it was a working foundry until 2003.

First and Florida ❸ may be a fairly nondescript intersection today, but it has played an enormous role in Milwaukee's economic history. With plenty of land, an abundance of nearby workers, and easy access to rail and water transportation, Walker's Point became Milwaukee's industrial incubator in the later 1800s, and this intersection was its epicenter. The pioneer was Edward P. Allis, who opened his Reliance Works on the southeast corner in 1867 and proceeded to make sawmill machinery, flour milling equipment, and the largest steam engines on earth. His creation evolved into Allis-Chalmers, which became one of the world's largest heavy equipment manufacturers after moving to (where else?) West Allis in 1902. Other enterprises followed the Reliance Works to Walker's Point, including Harnischfeger (overhead cranes), Nordberg (marine diesels and mine hoists), Kearney & Trecker (machine tools), A.O. Smith (car frames), Allen-Bradley (industrial controls), Filer & Stowell (sawmills), Chain Belt (belt drives), Vilter (refrigeration machinery), and Ladish (forgings). Every one of these industries became a giant in its field, and they all started within two blocks of First and Florida between 1867 and 1902—a world-class explosion of talent, energy, and innovation in an extraordinarily small space and time span. Walker's Point was in some important ways the Silicon Valley of its era.

## *Turn right on Bruce St. and left on S. 3rd St.*

The early industries are largely gone, but many of Walker's Point's early houses are still here. The neighborhood's residential district begins on Third Street with a row of distinctive homes from the late 1860s and 1870s. A lake captain owned the brick beauty at 634; it's crowned by a cupola known as a widow's walk, supposedly because a mariner's wife could look out over the harbor to see if her husband's ship had come in or sunk and left her a widow.

The venerable brick church across the field to your right was built by German Catholics in 1850 as Holy Trinity, the first Catholic church on the South Side. It is now **Holy Trinity-Our Lady of Guadalupe,** ❹ a center of worship for local Latino families.

In the next block, the concrete fortress at 710 was for decades the home of Junior House, a prominent women's garment manufacturer. In yet another instance of the neighborhood's transformation, the building became **Junior House Lofts** ❺ in 2013, featuring "Brooklyn style" apartments in an "industrial chic" setting.

Directly across the street is **Bradley Technical High School,** ❻ the 2003 successor to Boys Tech as the public school system's vocational/technical institution. The two schools have prepared generations of young people for skilled jobs in Milwaukee's trades and industries.

*The Allis Reliance Works was one of Milwaukee's largest industries and a catalyst for Walker's Point's development as a world-class manufacturing center.*

Crossing National Avenue, you enter a purely residential district that is among the best-preserved in the city. The homes on the right at 803, 813, and 821, sometimes called "**the mansions of Hanover Street**," ❼ represent a pinnacle of early South Side wealth. They were built in the 1870s for a railway engineer, a wine and liquor wholesaler, and a lumber merchant, respectively. The dominant theme in the blocks to the south is variety. Virtually no two homes are alike, and they represent economic diversity as well; cramped cottages share the street with much more spacious homes.

Diversity is also the keynote of Walker's Point's ethnic history. No Milwaukee neighborhood had a more cosmopolitan population in the 1800s. Its early residents included Yankee, German, Czech, Irish, and even Norwegian families. More typically associated with the rural Midwest, many Norwegians were skilled sailors, shipbuilders, and fishermen who naturally settled in the neighborhood closest to the city's waterfront. As Milwaukee industrialized in the later 1800s, more groups joined the procession: Serbs, Croats, Slovenes, Greeks, Poles, Bulgarians, and others from southern and eastern Europe. Nearly every group built its own churches, often more than one, which is why Walker's Point has the city's highest concentration of nineteenth-century religious buildings today. Its skyline is a virtual thicket of steeples.

The group with the greatest cultural impact on Walker's Point spoke Spanish as its native tongue. In the early 1920s, labor agents from the tanneries on the northern fringe of the neighborhood traveled to Mexico in search of workers. Hundreds of men responded, settling in the shadow of the tanneries and eventually sending for their families. The Latino population grew with the local economy, swelling to nearly 4000 by 1930; Milwaukee's Near South Side became by far the largest Spanish-speaking community in the state. With the arrival of Puerto Ricans after World War II, the barrio developed internal diversity of its own. Latinos of all backgrounds made up 20 percent of the city's population in 2020, and Walker's Point is the community's heart. Practically every church in neighborhood features a Latino-centered ministry, and dozens of social service organizations have been established. The **Guadalupe Head Start Center,**❽ housed in a former telephone exchange on Third and Washington, offers programs for the community's youngest Latinos.

Although its dominant accent is Spanish, Walker's Point remains a study in diversity. Gay and straight, Latino and Anglo, the neighborhood's residents are united by their appreciation of different cultures and their love of historic homes.

### Pull over at Greenfield Ave.

The mammoth industrial complex around you is **Rockwell Automation,**❾ successor to the Allen-Bradley Company. The enterprise was founded in 1903 by two mechanically inclined brothers, Lynde and Harry Bradley, who dropped out of high school to pursue their own design for a better motor controller. After a long period of trial and error, Allen-Bradley became a world leader in industrial controls. The company is the only founding Walker's Point industry that stayed in the neighborhood, developing a campus that today covers nearly seven square blocks. Its crowning glory is a clock tower first illuminated in 1962. For fifty years it was the largest four-faced clock on earth, but a bigger timepiece in Saudi Arabia necessitated a new title: largest in the Western Hemisphere.

Allen-Bradley's success attracted the attention of Rockwell International, which purchased the firm in 1985 and made it one of the largest manufacturers of factory automation equipment in the world. The current plant represents a paradigm shift in the global economy. Where thousands of blue-collar union workers once turned out switches, relays, and transistors by the ton, no one manufactures anything today. Rockwell still has thousands of employees in Walker's Point, but they tend to be software designers, marketers, accountants, IT experts, and other professionals. Production facilities are elsewhere, many of them overseas.

### Continue past Greenfield Ave. and turn right on Mitchell St.

*Young Mexican men began to flock to Walker's Point in the 1920s …*

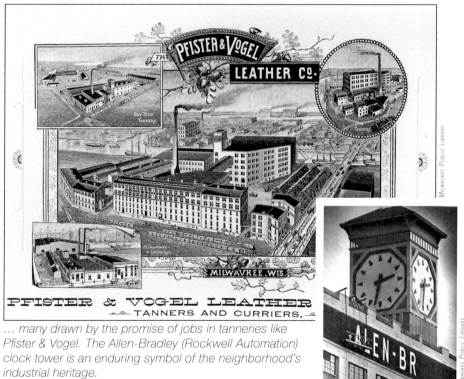

*… many drawn by the promise of jobs in tanneries like Pfister & Vogel. The Allen-Bradley (Rockwell Automation) clock tower is an enduring symbol of the neighborhood's industrial heritage.*

# Historic South Side

Greenfield Avenue is the southern border of Walker's Point. There are fewer historic homes in the next few blocks of Third Street, and most of them were built for industrial workers who walked to jobs at Allen-Bradley and other local employers. You have entered a neighborhood variously known as the Historic South Side, the Fourteenth Ward, or simply Polonia, the term for any Polish community outside Poland. If Walker's Point has always been a stronghold of diversity, this neighborhood was quite the opposite. One ethnic group—Poles—was dominant in the beginning, and another group—Latinos—is dominant today.

By 1900 Milwaukee's Polish community was second only to the city's German population in size. Its most important institution was **St. Stanislaus Catholic Church**, ❶ the twin-spired building yawning over the freeway that displaced hundreds of its parishioners. Founded in 1866, "St. Stan's" was the first Polish church in any American city and the mother parish of more than twenty Polish congregations scattered around Milwaukee, particularly on the South Side. The landmark has been completely restored since 2015 as a center for celebration of the Latin Mass, and it draws Catholic traditionalists from throughout the region.

St. Stan's also anchors the east end of the Mitchell Street commercial district. Just as N. Third Street was the German community's downtown, Mitchell played the same role for South Side Poles. Its skyline is still comparable to what you'll see in a medium-sized city like Fond du Lac or Sheboygan. As the surrounding area's accent changed from Polish to Spanish, Latino merchants multiplied, but you can also find Indian, Pakistani, and Syrian establishments on Mitchell today.

Some of the street's original mainstays have been put to other uses. Kunzelmann-Esser on Seventh, once famous for its "Nine Floors of Fine Furniture," has been converted to loft apartments. **St. Anthony Church** ❷ on Ninth was every bit as Catholic as St. Stanislaus, just four blocks away, but it was founded in 1872 by Germans, and never the two shall meet. It's a Latino parish today, and sponsor of one of the largest Catholic grade schools in America, with multiple campuses on the South Side. Directly across the street from St. Anthony is the old Hill's Department Store, which was converted to a Milwaukee Public Library branch in 2017, with apartments on the upper floors. Filling the entire block between Tenth and Eleventh is the third Schuster's Department Store you've seen on this tour, the South Side counterpart of stores on Vliet Street and King Drive. One block west, at Twelfth, is the **Modjeska Theater,** ❸ built in 1924 and named for a famous Polish actress. Once the grandest movie palace on the South Side, the Modjeska patiently awaits a rebirth. Bridal shops were a Mitchell Street specialty for decades, and there are still one or two west of Twelfth. They have found a new market as outfitters for *quinceañeras*, the elaborate ceremonies that celebrate a fifteen-year-old Latina's passage to womanhood.

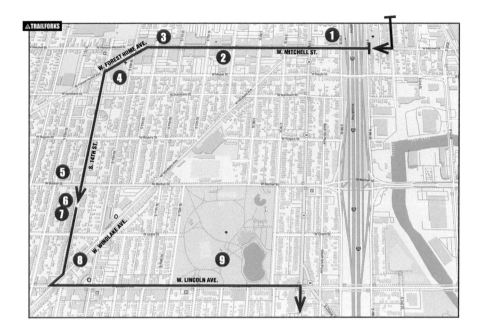

## Turn diagonally left on Forest Home Ave.

**Sears, Roebuck & Co.** ❹ built the store on your left in 1928, when the mail-order giant was fast becoming a department store giant. Sears was an instant success here and kept on growing through the post-World War II era. The parking lot was so busy in the 1950s that a traffic controller was perched in a tower with a loudspeaker to direct motorists to available spaces. The store was shuttered in 1983 as part of a national retrenchment. It is now owned by the Villarreals, an entrepreneurial Mexican family who have developed a thriving chain of food stores and tortilla factories under the brand name El Rey—"The King." Mitchell Street is no longer the South Side's downtown but, as the Villarreals' success demonstrates, it is still a lively center of commerce.

## Turn left on S. 14th St.

The residential area south of Mitchell Street was the heart of the old Fourteenth Ward, once the most densely settled ward in the city. Milwaukee's Poles were as poor as any nineteenth-century immigrant group, but they came to America with an intense desire to own their own homes. That desire reflected the traditional peasant belief that land meant security; money can burn and animals can die, but land is forever. As a result, the immigrants covered block after block south of Mitchell Street with painfully small houses shoehorned onto thirty-foot lots.

*Mary Heft, my grandmother, as a young woman on S. 14th Street*

*Her neighborhood was a compact cluster of modest homes, most of them Polish flats.*

*Mitchell Street was the South Side's "downtown" for generations.*

They founded Catholic churches as they spread south. In fact, you can chart the growth of the South Side Polonia by following its church steeples. The one to the right on Becher Street belongs to **St. Hyacinth,❺** a parish established in 1883. Today, reflecting the neighborhood's changed demographics, the sign above the main entrance to St. Hyacinth incorporates both *Witamy* and *Bienvenidos*—"Welcome" in Polish and Spanish.

### Pull over at 2135 S. 14th St.

The Historic South Side's homes may be small, but they tell an oversized story. Many are of a type known locally as the **Polish flat.❻** The house at 2135 S. 14th is a good example, as are the classic Polish flats at 2134, 2140, and 2142. Their earmarks are steep front steps and at-grade windowsills on the lower level; residents could look out and see their mailman's knees. To understand the origin of the Polish flat, you have to imagine these houses perhaps five feet shorter than they are today. The first home on each lot was typically a basementless cottage supported by cedar posts. As the years passed and they saved enough money, the homeowners would jack up their cottages with heavy-duty industrial jacks and use brick or block to create a half-basement living unit beneath the first. Building in stages—a practice scholars call "additive architecture"—allowed the immigrants to own as much house as they could as soon as they could. It was a rather ingenious way to double their living space; building a second unit on top of the first would have been far more expensive than raising the cottage and adding rooms beneath it.

The Polish flat's impact was multiple. It encouraged multi-generational living, first of all; often the first son or daughter to get married would move downstairs and start a new family. It could also be a welcome source of income; the lower units were frequently rented to new immigrants seeking a foothold in the company of people who spoke their language. But perhaps its most important impact was psychological. In the Old World, the Polish peasants were worlds away from the landed gentry. In Milwaukee, they could buy that little thirty-foot lot and instantly become landowners. If they built a cottage, turned it into a Polish flat, and rented the lower unit, they were land *lords* as well. Few Milwaukee house types tell such a compelling story, and this neighborhood is full of them.

One of the stories belongs to my grandmother, who was born Mary Heft in 1892. She was the fourth of six children raised by Polish immigrants right here at **2137 S. Fourteenth.❼** Her father died of tuberculosis when she was eight, leaving her mother to raise her brood on a washerwoman's wages. The children might easily have ended up in an orphanage; there was no social safety net in those days, and the loss of a breadwinner often meant the collapse of a family. What kept the Hefts together was the fact that they owned five living units on this little thirty-foot lot: three in the front house and two in the backyard cottage. They lived in the smallest unit, of course, upstairs and in the rear of the front house. The others were rented, which enabled my grandmother's family to not only stay together but to purchase one of the first pianos in the neighborhood, a point of particular pride.

With so many small units on so many small lots, it's easy to see why this neighborhood was the city's densest. When Mary Heft was growing up here, the five households on her single lot had a combined total of twenty-seven children. That's enough for three baseball teams! She walked up the block every day to St. Hyacinth School, where the typical classroom had 100 students, taught by a single nun.

We wouldn't tolerate those densities today, and they raised obvious public health concerns, but the sheer mass of humanity here created an incredibly strong sense of place and a powerful spirit of group identity. If you grew up in the Fourteenth Ward, you knew who you were. Today the neighborhood is largely Latino, and most of the half-basement living units have become conventional basements, but the tradition of ethnic solidarity is no less potent for the area's current residents than it was for the first.

### Continue on 14th St., turn right on Windlake Ave., and turn immediately left on Lincoln Ave.

Another architectural holdover in this and many other old Milwaukee neighborhoods is corner businesses. Long before shopping malls and big-box retailers existed, the city's commerce was intensely local; its residential areas were dotted with bakeries, butcher shops, hardware stores, tailor shops, grocery stores, and saloons, which famously played a role as "the workingman's club." The vast majority of corner commercial buildings have been converted to other uses, most often housing, but they remain distinctive features in the urban landscape.

Windlake Avenue's ❽ diagonal orientation signals that it's an old farm-to-market road, one that predates the urban street grid that now locks it in a cage of right angles. In the mid-1800s, Milwaukee developed a network of plank roads, oversized wooden sidewalks that made straight-line connections with settlements in outstate Wisconsin. They're paved today, but the diagonal roads are still here, and their names tell you where they went. On the South Side, Windlake Avenue led to Wind Lake, Muskego Avenue to Muskego, and Beloit Road to Beloit. The same pattern is evident in even larger diagonal streets north of the Menomonee Valley, including Lisbon Avenue, Green Bay Avenue, Appleton Avenue, and Fond du Lac Avenue.

Lincoln Avenue was never a regional downtown like Mitchell Street, but it was an important neighborhood shopping district, and the street still offers some interesting specialties. A&J Polish Deli, at 1215 Lincoln, is a throwback to the area's original ethnic heritage, with plenty of *kluski, kielbasa,* and *kiszona kapusta* (noodles, sausage, and sauerkraut) for sale. If you stop by on a Saturday morning, the language you're most likely to hear spoken is Polish. Ben's Cycle, at 1013, is a full-service bicycle shop meeting the two-wheeled needs of a regional clientele; the shop is now in its third generation of Hanoski family ownership. Establishments like Tres Hermanos Restaurant, Durango Western Wear, and El Lucero Liquor are more typical Lincoln Avenue businesses today.

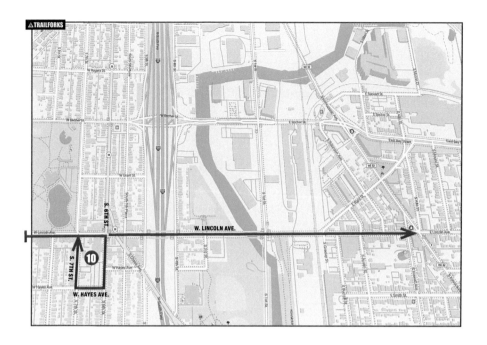

*The statue of Polish and American military hero Gen. Tadeusz Kosciuszko stands guard over the park that bears his name.*

*St. Josaphat's Basilica is a monument to the faith of the Polish immigrants who built it.*

**Kosciuszko Park,** ❾ which starts at Tenth Street, is the Historic South Side's largest public green space. It was named for Gen. Tadeusz Kosciuszko, a Polish nobleman who crossed the ocean to help the American colonies win their independence from England. His statue, completely restored in 2013, stands at Ninth Place. A military architect by trade, Kosciuszko designed the first fortifications at West Point and earned the rank of brigadier general in the Continental Army. He also became a good friend of Thomas Jefferson, whom he named as the executor of his will. Kosciuszko directed that his American estate be sold to free and educate slaves—a provision that was never carried out. Wherever there are Poles in America, you'll find parks, streets, and other landmarks named for the general. If you want to impress your Polish friends, by the way, pronounce his name Kosh-CHOO-shko" (as in "cash check") rather than the more commonly used "Kozzy-ESS-ko," or "Kozzy" for short.

*Circle St. Josaphat's Basilica by turning right on 6th St., right on Hayes St., right on 7th St., and right again to return to Lincoln Ave and continue eastward.*

Diagonally across from the park is the largest church in the city: **St. Josaphat's Basilica.**🔟 This is my favorite Milwaukee building, not only for its aesthetic grandeur but for the story it tells of aspiration, struggle, and ultimate triumph. St. Josaphat's Parish was founded in 1888 as the city's fifth Polish congregation, with a fairly modest starter church on Lincoln Avenue. As immigrants poured into the neighborhood, the building was soon hopelessly overcrowded. Within a decade St. Josaphat's had roughly 12,000 members, making it probably the largest congregation of any faith in the entire state. Knowing that even more newcomers were on the way, Father Wilhelm Grutza, the pastor, hired a German-born architect named Erhard Brielmaier to design what is basically a scaled-down version of St. Peter's in Rome.

Brielmaier's plans called for brick and terra cotta structure, but Father Grutza, on a brick-buying trip to Chicago, learned that the Chicago Post Office and Custom House was being torn down. Spying a bargain, Grutza bought the entire structure for a reported $20,000, then had it disassembled and shipped north to Milwaukee on some 500 flatcars. The architect didn't flinch. Brielmaier simply redrew his plans to incorporate the gorgeous sandstone blocks and proceeded to give Milwaukee one of the greenest buildings in its history. The church is constructed almost completely of recycled materials, right down to the big brass Post Office doorknobs bearing the seal of the United States.

Ground was broken in 1896, and the church was dedicated in 1901. Although it nearly bankrupted the parishioners, their new home is still the closest thing in Wisconsin to a genuine European cathedral. Its structural steel dome was also second in size only to the one on the U.S. Capitol. In 1929, after the interior work was finally completed, Pope Pius XI declared St. Josaphat's a basilica, a mark of special honor in the Catholic Church—a little like being named to the ecclesiastical all-star team.

By the time the parish reached its century mark in 1988, the building was showing its age. The dome leaked, plaster was falling, and the glorious stained-glass windows were starting to sag. In 1990 the nonprofit, nonsectarian St. Josaphat Basilica Foundation was formed to address those and other problems. The group has so far raised and spent more than $10 million to completely restore the building, from the cross on the cupola to the chapel in the basement. It's a remarkable success story. If you have the time and you're here during business hours, you can see the results for yourself on a self-guided audio tour of the basilica. Enter through the St. John Paul II Pavilion on the Seventh Street side.

Continuing east on Lincoln Avenue, you enter a long buffer zone between two notable neighborhoods. Interstate 94, acres of parkland, and the mighty Kinnickinnic River (Milwaukee's smallest) separate the Historic South Side from the last neighborhood you'll visit: Bay View.

# Bay View

Bay View began as a company town built around an iron mill established on the lakefront in 1868. The Milwaukee Iron Company quickly became the second-largest maker of railroad rails in America and the largest employer in Milwaukee, with a multi-ethnic work force that exceeded 1500 during peak periods. In 1879, with a major push from the mill's owners, Bay View incorporated as the city's first suburb. It was an unusually self-contained community, but Milwaukee soon reached the village's northern border right here on Lincoln Avenue. City residents north of Lincoln enjoyed running water, sewer service, and streetlights while Bay Viewites made do with wells, backyard privies, and kerosene lamps. In 1887, against the clearly expressed wishes of mill management, local residents voted overwhelmingly to consolidate with the city. A village became a neighborhood, but it was like getting married and keeping your name. This is still Bay View, and it has one of the most robust community identities in the Milwaukee area.

### *Turn right on Kinnickinnic Avenue.*

The Bay View business district begins in earnest at the **Kinnickinnic-Lincoln-Howell triangle.**❶ Kinnickinnic Avenue itself began as an Indian trail and became one of those farm-to-market roads that took a somewhat crooked path to the countryside. The Bay View neighborhood has become a darling of developers in the twenty-first century, and Kinnickinnic is its Main Street, with a full menu of restaurants, nightspots, and specialty shops that have all opened since 2000. One of the most unusual destinations is the **Avalon Theater** ❷ at 2473 Kinnickinnic. A neighborhood fixture since 1929, the Avalon is one of Milwaukee's last "atmospheric" movie palaces; its interior evokes a Spanish courtyard on a summer evening, with stars actually twinkling in the ceiling overhead.

Crossing Potter Avenue, you enter a stretch of Kinnickinnic sometimes referred to as **"beautiful downtown Bay View."** ❸ The storefronts are more concentrated here, and the restaurants more abundant.

### *Turn left on Russell Ave.*

The church on the corner as you turn is **Immaculate Conception,**❹ which everyone in Bay View calls simply "IC." Founded in 1871 by Irish Catholics who worked in the mill, it was a very insular community. When Italians were drawn to the neighborhood by jobs in the same mill, they were not welcome to worship here. In Milwaukee and elsewhere, diversity did not always mean harmony.

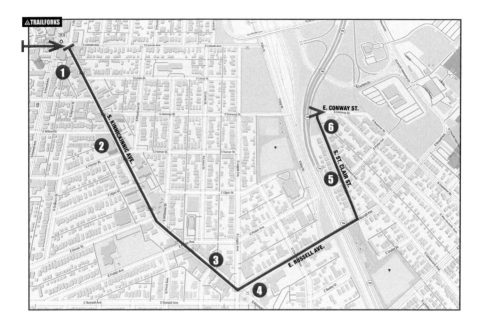

## Turn left on St. Clair St.

Passing under the Lake Parkway just east of Bay Street, you enter the heart of the old company town. This area was developed by the Milwaukee Iron Company in an effort to attract workers to what was then a relatively remote location. They came in large numbers, including a sizable contingent from the iron-working regions of England. The skilled workers unionized early, forming the Sons of Vulcan in 1873. Their headquarters was **Puddlers Hall** ❺ at 2461 St. Clair. Now a popular tavern, it was named for one of the mill's skilled trades. The Sons of Vulcan were a predecessor of today's United Steelworkers International, and their hall is among the oldest and best-preserved union landmarks in the Midwest.

## Turn right on Conway St. and pull over.

To the right is one of my favorite Milwaukee restaurants, **Three Brothers**, ❻ which was built in 1897 as a saloon that sold only Schlitz products. Bay View's mill workers developed prodigious thirsts in the course of their ten- to twelve-hour days; there was another Schlitz "tied house" just three blocks away, and a variety of other saloons in the area sold competitors' products. Remarkably, the original Schlitz globe still crowns the turret above the main entrance of Three Brothers. The saloon became a restaurant in 1956, and it is now in its third generation of Radicevic family ownership. The dishes served here are authentically Serbian, a cuisine influenced by Turkey and Greece but uniquely its own.

To your left is the **site of the Bay View iron mill.**❼ It made different products under different owners over the years, but the mill remained one of Milwaukee's largest employers and heaviest industries. The complex covered nearly thirty acres on the south lakefront, and the flames from its gigantic blast furnace lit up the night sky over Bay View for decades. The glow was extinguished in 1929. United States Steel was the mill's owner at the time, and the conglomerate had centralized production in its mammoth complex in Gary, Indiana. The Bay View plant became a "scrap mill," kept busy with short runs and odd jobs until it ground to a halt in the same year the stock market crashed. The city and the steel company bickered for nearly a decade about the fate of the property, but it ultimately entered the public domain as passively managed park land.

The mill is still remembered as the site of the bloodiest labor disturbance in Wisconsin's history. On May 5, 1886, a crowd of roughly 1500 striking workers, most of them Polish immigrants, marched on the rolling mill as part of a nation-wide movement for the eight-hour day without a cut in pay. They found the militia waiting for them. At a distance of 200 yards, the troops opened fire, killing seven marchers, including a thirteen-year-old schoolboy who was apparently playing hooky. The shootings quelled the eight-hour movement but also galvanized the strikers to organize politically, paving the way for the phenomenal success of the worker-oriented Socialist Party in the following decades.

When you look out over the site today, it's hard to believe that such an enormous industrial enterprise ever existed in Bay View. If you look in the opposite direction, however, the mill is still here, because the neighborhood is in every sense its creation. If this had been raw land awaiting Milwaukee's expansion, it might easily have become a twin of the city's Upper East Side, a haven for affluent residents attracted by the panoramic views of the lake. The fact that Bay View had an industrial character years before the city grew out to meet it has continuing relevance today.

## *Turn right on Wentworth Ave.*

Mill workers' houses from the 1870s and later tend to be modest indeed, but they have attracted a great deal of interest from homeseekers looking for vintage architecture ten minutes from downtown. Bay View has become a hotbed of preservation activity, and the area around the mill is one of its epicenters. This was **Bay View's Little Italy** ❽ for many years. Unlike the heavily Sicilian Third Ward, however, immigrants from northern and central Italy were dominant here.

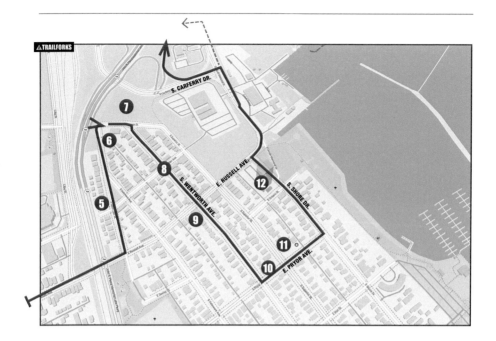

One of the most durable Italian landmarks is **Groppi's Market** ❾ on Wentworth and Russell Avenues. Established in 1913, it sold work clothes and live chickens as well as imported pasta and homemade Italian sausage. This was the boyhood home of Father James Groppi. His family was among those who were shunned at Immaculate Conception and had to travel to Our Lady of Pompeii in the Third Ward for their weddings and funerals. That shared experience of prejudice helped to shape the values and the viewpoint of one of Milwaukee's most important civil rights leaders.

## Turn left on Pryor Ave.

On your left is the last **public well** ❿ in Milwaukee. It was one of Bay View's primary water sources during the village period, and it continues to flow, although the artesian pressure from the early years has been supplanted by an electric pump. The well is popular among Milwaukeeans who prefer untreated water for themselves and especially for their plants.

The fine Victorian home at 2590 S. Superior Street was built in 1872 for mill executive Warren Brinton and his wife Beulah. Mrs. Brinton became Bay View's den mother, in a sense, with a particular affection for the immigrant families who depended on the mill. She let them use her tennis court, taught them how to sew, and started the community's first library. The **Beulah Brinton house** ⓫ is now the home of the Bay View Historical Society, the only neighborhood-based historical society in the state. The depth of the past in Bay View is profound, and so is the depth of feeling for the community's heritage.

*Turn left on South Shore Dr.*

You are now in the 2500 South block overlooking the lake. Try to visualize what the comparable block of 2500 North looked like. You were in the North Point neighborhood, surrounded by homes designed by architects for some of Milwaukee's wealthiest families. Most of the houses on Shore Drive were built for people who walked to jobs in one of the grimiest industries in Wisconsin. The view is the same, and access is better because the bluffs aren't as high, but the two areas could hardly be more different: castles to the north, cottages to the south. Once again, history is why things are the way they are, and it's glaringly obvious in the landscape of Bay View.

The high-rise at the north end of Shore Drive is called **Bay View Terrace.** 🄬 Completed in 1964, it was planned as a condominium project, but no one could even spell the word at the time; it opened as an apartment tower. Although Bay View's alderman, Erwin Zillman, considered the Terrace a welcome sign of things to come, his constituents vehemently disagreed. They packed a City Hall hearing room to demand a zoning change that made any further high-rise developments illegal. Converted to condos in 1980, Bay View Terrace offers spectacular views, but it will remain one of a kind for the foreseeable future.

### *Turn right on Russell Ave. and follow the signs to Interstate 794.*

Russell Avenue marks the south end of the mill property, which has long since been converted to other uses, all of them distinctly non-residential. The mothballed Naval and Marine Reserve Center is on the left, Milwaukee's Coast Guard station on the right, and the Lake Express ferry complex just up the shoreline.

*If you're on a bicycle, continue north to the Lincoln Avenue bridge and follow it over the railroad tracks to Bay Street. Bay, Kinnickinnic Avenue, and S. First Street will take you back to downtown Milwaukee.*

**If you're driving, turn left one block sooner on Carferry Drive, pass the Port of Milwaukee's administration building, and get on the Dan Hoan Bridge.**

*Bay View developed as a company town built around a massive iron mill on the south lakefront.*

*Many of its early residents worked ten- to twelve-hour days in temperatures approaching 160 degrees.*

The bridge follows the spine of the heavy-duty peninsula known as **Jones Island.** 🔞 Today the "Island" is the site of Milwaukee's sewage treatment plant and port facilities, as well as petroleum storage tanks and piles of road salt, but Jones Island was once the center of commercial fishing in the region. From the 1870s until the 1920s, it supported a colony of fishing families from the Baltic seacoast of Poland—a group called the Kaszubs—who brought up two million pounds of fish in a typical year. Their rustic settlement peaked at 1600 residents, but most were evicted in the 1920s to make way for today's developments.

The **Hoan Bridge** 🔞 itself has an interesting history. Named for the Socialist who served as Milwaukee's mayor from 1916 to 1940, it was part of the planned Lake Freeway, which would have bulldozed through Juneau Park on the north end and taken more than 500 homes and businesses on the south. Intense opposition surfaced on both sides, but there was no one in the middle, on Jones Island, to object, and so Milwaukee County proceeded to build a bridge to federal freeway standards. Completed in 1974, it was the famous "bridge to nowhere" for three long years. The span was finally connected to surface streets in 1977, and in 1999 the Lake Parkway provided a high-speed outlet to the south.

However checkered its history, the Hoan Bridge offers sweeping views of the landscapes you've experienced at ground level today. You can see how St. Josaphat's Basilica towers over the neighborhood it rose from. You can appreciate the dominance of the twin spires of St. Stanislaus Church and the Rockwell Automation clock tower. The thicket of steeples in the multi-ethnic Walker's Point neighborhood is plainly apparent, and you have an unusual bird's-eye view of both the Third Ward's condos and the Summerfest grounds. Framing the entire ensemble on the east is the magnificent lake that sparked the creation of the city in the first place.

*Stay in the right lane and take the Michigan Street exit to return to the lakefront and end your tour.*

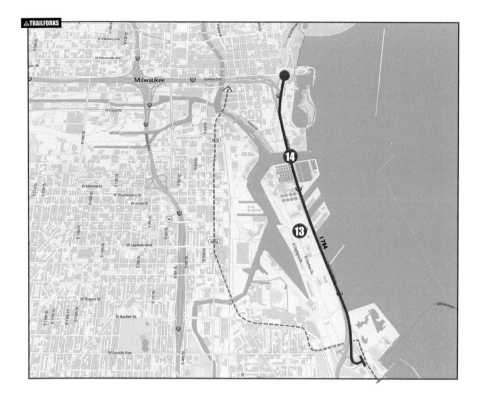

I t may be self-evident, but you've spent the better part of your day in what is often referred to as the central city. That term might call up an image of crime, congestion, and squalor, but I hope you've seen at least two things in your close-up view of Milwaukee. The first is the city's diversity. There is a remarkable variety of worlds in this particular urban world, and together they give the community a cosmopolitan vibrancy that is one of its primary assets. The second is Milwaukee's vitality. However challenged some of its neighborhoods, however much in need of new resources, there is no place you've seen today that is without fresh energy and continuing hope.

*John Gurda's Milwaukee* is, of course, everyone's Milwaukee. If you're a visitor, I hope you've enjoyed this grassroots introduction to a unique American city. If you're a resident, whether your ancestors shopped at Solomon Juneau's trading post or you moved here last week, I hope the tour has enriched your experience of Milwaukee as home. This is a manageable city, a community built at the human scale, and there's a great deal more to see. The route you've followed today is just one thread in a densely woven urban fabric. I hope it has whetted your appetite to make discoveries of your own. Grow where you're planted. Love where you live.